Review

"Adel has written a very comprehensive, step-by-step guide for sales professionals. The APWS selling method, outlined in his book, includes a wide range of communication techniques which guide the reader to effectively communicate with potential customers and close more deals."

"As a communication consultant, I was interested in how Adel focuses on building the relationship - developing awareness, clarifying needs and desires, building chemistry and helping the customer more deeply understand the potential value of the product or service being offered."

"His extensive index allows the reader to use the guide effectively on an as-needed basis. It is filled with processes, explanations and examples of how to apply them in a variety of situations while selling diverse products and services."

"I would recommend this guide to any sales professional looking to up their game, refine their sales skills and explore a set of tools and approaches that will support them in reaching their career potential."

Heather Chetwynd
Director and Principal Trainer
Voice to Word Consulting Inc.
VoiceToWord.ca

$APWS
$ELLING

Awareness-Pinpoint Questions-Wish Creation-Support Intervention

THE MOST EFFECTIVE SALES METHOD
USED FOR OVER 57000 SALES CALLS

ADEL WILLIAMS

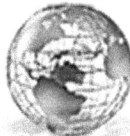

START PROFESSIONAL
PUBLISHING INC., MILTON,
ONTARIO, CANADA

Contents

Preface

Sales professionals often find themselves losing sleep at night, stumped as to how to meet their sales targets when faced with the ever-present dual challenges of stiff market competition and customers whose behavior and priorities are sometimes difficult and certainly highly diverse. They've done everything right – or so they think – yet the purchase orders just aren't coming in. Sometimes they can't even get a face-to-face appointment with prospective customers. At other times, they've lost customers, despite having the superior product/pricing. Eventually they have to ask themselves: Am I doing something wrong? Is there another way to reach my sales targets while making the selling process smooth and stress-free?

In *Sales Excellence Using the APWS Selling Method,* readers discover the key elements that must be addressed for almost any sale to be successful. Moreover, this book describes a new and proven approach to selling – wish creation – an approach that has been absent from previous books about professional selling. While the pharmaceutical and medical devices industry is the backdrop for this new selling approach, the guidelines offered in *Sales Excellence Using the APWS Selling Method* can be successfully applied to selling in almost any industry because they tap into the core issues that underlie every buying decision: customer needs and wishes.

Despite years of sales education and close study of existing books on the topic of selling, my own professional experience and success have come from a novel approach to selling, one which has not, to my knowledge, been described elsewhere. After decades of sales experience in the pharmaceutical and medical devices industry and based on 57,000 sales calls analysis, APWS selling method has been developed as a novel and reliable approach to selling. It addresses every situation that a sales representative faces, every type of customer, and every challenging situation, from customers who have turned their backs on a company to customers who are loyal to a company or its products. The APWS Selling Method teaches readers how to word their questions so as to secure the desired response, how to contend with challenging questions and personalities so as to inspire trust and overcome biases, and how to ensure that product demos and trials lead to a purchase order from a pleased customer.

Among the special features of this book are, as previously noted, my unique approach to selling both to the customer's need, and, when applicable, to the customer's wishes. Readers learn how best to approach customers based on the customer's personality type, and how best to approach customers in each of a variety of situations. These situations include customers who may be:

- unaware of the need for a superior product
- selling/using/prescribing a competitor's product
- habituated to using an inferior product or solution despite the extra work, costs, or hazards that accompany it
- unaware that they are expending precious funds on maintenance costs for products when maintenance-free products are available and would free up their budget for other items
- unaware that a superior product is available and will benefit them/their facility/patients

The APWS Selling Method provides readers with many new sales techniques. These include:

- The *APWS Selling Method* (Awareness, Pinpoint questions, Wish creation, Support Intervention)
- A new technique for asking probing questions by using *Pinpoint questions*

- A new model for building an *attention grabber* using the *APWS Selling Method*
- A new, step-by-step model for *rapport-building*
- A new model for handling indifferent personalities *(the APOC approach)*
- An *objection-solving technique*
- How to sell to customers who are using a direct *competitor's products*
- Classification of *personalities and behaviors*
- Guidelines for breaking *customer : problem bonds*
- A new product presentation model: *FIOV* (feature, impact, outcome, value)
- A new sales approach for *healthcare products*
- A *new leadership model* for sales professionals and sales managers.

Once you've learned the APWS Selling Method, and learned the best way to approach the various customer personalities and how to deal with every possible selling situation, you'll be well on your way to meeting and likely exceeding your sales targets each year. So, let's get started!

1
What is the sales process?

A sales process is an intervention for a solution, and results in a win - win situation in which customer problems are identified and resolved through a product's or a service's value. Multiple successful sales processes result in achieving sales forecasts and increase the profits for your organization.

The process required to successfully close a professional sales call is not obvious, but once you understand and apply the principles in this book, it will be an easy task. Four of the most crucial tasks in the success of the sales call are building a rapport with customers, preparing for the sales calls, understanding your customer's practice including the obstacles they might be facing, and finally, communicating your message in a professional and clear manner. When sales professionals master these four tasks, the result will be a smooth close for the sale.

I was hired to be the sales and marketing director for a large laboratory group which was doing analytical product testing. The laboratory was selling and promoting our analytical testing services to pharmaceutical companies, cosmetic, and veterinary companies either for finished products or raw materials. I soon discovered that the lab was losing customers and sales were declining dramatically with the remaining customers. I visited one of the customers and used professional probing technique to learn about the problems. The customer mentioned that the main issue was a communication problem. The customer had been asked to send a specific number of samples to the lab and then the results took longer than usual to be available. Only when the customer called to follow-up on her results did she learn that there were not enough samples.

There were three issues here. First, the lab miscommunicated the number of samples required, asking for nine units containing three samples each (for a total of 27 samples). The lab assumed that the customer knew that each unit required three samples. The lab told the customer to send nine units and the customer sent nine, but there was only one sample in each of her nine units (for a total of 9 samples).

The second issue was that, once the lab realized there weren't enough samples, it didn't inform the customer until the customer called the lab wondering why the results were late in arriving.

The third issue was that the lab didn't visit the customer to address the situation or offer an apology for miscommunicating.

Challenges in this situation:

- Needs of the laboratory were not clearly communicated to the customer.
- Lack of communication.
- No corrective action has been made.

For these reasons, the customer decided to bring her business to another laboratory to avoid any delay in getting the results based on future samples. In this example we need to learn that needs have to be clearly identified by asking the right questions.

When you receive a P.O. (purchase order) don't leave your customer wondering what's going on. Maintain contact with your customers and update them about the steps you are taking to get their work done.

Reflecting on the previous example, if the lab had sent a follow-up email upon receiving the samples and noted that there were not enough samples, the matter would have been resolved easily and promptly.

When you get a P.O. from a customer, don't assume that your job is over. In fact, your job has just started because now you want to retain that customer.

Preparation for your sales call

Preparing for your sales call is one of the most important steps in the sales process. Mastering this step along with the uncover step can guarantee 50% of your success in your sales call.

The preparation step is divided into distinct steps.

The first thing you do is to set an appointment with your customer. Don't walk in to the facility without an appointment. You need to get quality time with your customer. You want time to prepare, unrushed, for the appointment, to ensure it goes smoothly and effectively.

You can set up a 'lunch and learn' appointment, which works in your favor.

Prepare and bring all available information about the account.

1. In terms of preparation, the first thing you need to do is to study your product very well and study the competitor's products as well.
2. Ask more experienced members of the sales team how they approached sales calls for your product, what the common objections were and how they were handled?
3. Know what your product's strengths and weaknesses are; what are the precautions and side effects? Study your product's features, impacts, outcomes and related values for the patient and for the physician. Identify your competitor's weaknesses and strengths. Develop an in-depth understanding of all studies about your product. (You should get this information from your company product training and marketing department.)
4. Prepare for your opening, attention-grabber and probing questions.
5. Prepare for your position statement.
6. Anticipate common questions, objections and know how to answer/respond.
7. Prepare to deal with different personalities and behaviors.
8. Prepare the tools for your sales call, like literature, visual aids, samples, studies. Samples must be in a very good condition and not near their expiration date, and be well-packaged in brand-new condition.

9. Prepare information about your customer or prospect like his or her name, address, and specialty, his or her personality and attitude, how to build rapport and win her or his confidence and trust. Know what kind of products he prescribes. (You can get this information from the nearest pharmacy or from your company's CRM).

10. Prepare all information you need to gather from or share with the customer during your sales call.

11. Prepare for a commitment statement.

12. Role play with your colleagues before meeting with customers.

GOLDEN RULE, DON'T MAKE A CALL WHEN YOU ARE UPSET OR NOT IN THE MOOD. ALWAYS HAVE A POSITIVE ATTITUDE.

In your first product call, you have limited information about your customer. If you promote product **X**, you need to anticipate all possible customer reactions. Your customer might be prescribing product **A** for so many reasons, and might never have heard about your product due to lack of visits. He or she might have heard about your product, but your competitor is doing a good job selling the product, or your customer has a good relationship with your competitor's representative or your competitor's company management team.

> *"You've got to be very careful if you don't know where you are going, because you might not get there."*
>
> *Yogi Berra*

In my first job as a medical rep. in a pharmaceutical company, I had just completed my first training course ever on neuro products, cough sedatives, multivitamins and hypertensive drugs. Our field sales supervisor gave me and my colleagues product samples for a week's work in advance, and then directed me to visit a famous neurosurgeon who worked downtown. I left our company office, full of enthusiasm, with a bag full of samples for a week's work and went to meet the neurosurgeon at his office. To my surprise, he agreed to meet with me without an appointment. I was trying to make a sales call, but he interrupted me, asking, what's inside your bag?

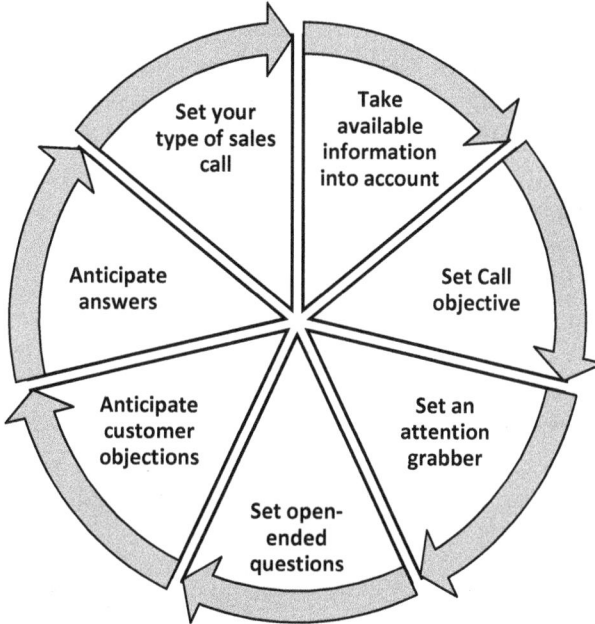

Pre-call planning Model

I told him it was full of various samples. He asked if he could see them. I started to sort through the samples to find the neuro samples, but he told me to open the bag and let him see what I had in it. I opened the bag, but he instead took it from my hands and turned it upside down on his desk dumping out around 70 samples. Then he handed my empty bag back and said, "Okay, thank you for the samples, now you can go as I am very busy."

Although I reacted calmly in front of him, I could barely see in front of me as I left his office feeling very hot and sweaty. I ran to our company office which was one kilometer away from his office, where my supervisor laughed and told me that the whole thing was planned as a test of self-control and to teach me what I really should have done before any visit. She said, "Welcome aboard", then she started giving me the first lesson in sales and I started to learn how to prepare for a successful sales call. I had expected that I was going to be fired before I even completed my second call, but fortunately that never happened!

What were the lessons from that experience?

1. I didn't prepare for the meeting and the call and didn't get enough information about my customer.
2. I didn't know what the customer needed, so I stumbled through the presentation.
3. I didn't build rapport with the customer.
4. I didn't plan for the weekly calls in advance, so my bag was poorly organized.
5. I didn't make an appointment, so he was in a rush to get the samples and end the meeting which didn't allow me to make my presentation.
6. I didn't script my presentation as a result I didn't grab my customer's attention.
7. I lost all my samples. Normally, reps only stock their bag with the samples needed for the people they are planning to meet on a given day.
8. I was not able to secure any commitment from the physician to prescribe our drugs, because I never had the chance to present the products to him as I should have.

That's a typical example of an unprepared sales representative but what kept me in the position is that I controlled my temper and my reaction to the situation.

My advice to new sales reps is to be very well-controlled under pressure. Never lose your temper and remain patient. In many sales situations, you will face aggression, skepticism, indifferent customer personalities and many other challenging behaviors. In this book, I offer you my support by teaching you how to deal with each of these challenges.

How customers make buying decisions

Before we dig more deeply into how to do a professional sales call, it's important to know how the customer makes a buying decision and which factors are important to the customer in making a buying decision.

- **Building relationship and confidence:**
  The best sales outcomes happen when you focus first on building rapport with your customer. In this process it's not about the value you bring to your customer but it's about how you make your customer feel. Would (s)he like to see you again? Create that level of comfort, chemistry and the feeling that 'we click'. Your sales call should be a balance between a relational and a scripted sales call. Physicians should feel that you are an ally, an important resource to them who supports them in their clinical practice.

  Some pharmaceutical companies have been focused on shifting towards this goal, which necessitates a move towards building a relationship first and then individualizing the sale to each particular doctor. One of the physicians explained the relationship as:

  > *"They learn about me and what I want to know and what matters to me."*

  When sales reps make an effort to create that relationship and confidence with their customers, they have a better chance at getting their prescriptions written.

  Some of the sales representatives who are considered good by doctors adapt their presentations to fit the personalities of those doctors and each doctor's interests, whether those interests are social or business. For example, doctors who are very interested in medicines that are covered by many insurance providers will want to hear more about the drug coverage in the selling pitch. Affordability is key in certain areas, depending on the doctor's specialty, clinic and location. One doctor specifically mentioned drug coverage saying this:

  > *"I always ask about cost, because a lot of the patients that I see can't afford some of the medicines. That must be forefront in my mind. Is this a brand-new drug that will be very expensive, and will not even be an option for my patient, or is it something that they will be able to reasonably afford?"*

- **Uncover existing outcome gaps:**
  Did the sales professional pinpointed the issues that the customer is suffering from? Has he been successful in identifying the customer's pain? Customers trust sales professionals who are able to detect their issues and they come to consider them sales advisors.

- **Extra feature's impact, outcome and value compared to what the customer is presently using:**
  There is a big difference between providing a piece of information and adding value. Remember that every product has a feature, impact, corresponding outcome and value. Usually the customer evaluates the product in terms of extra value. It's very hard to sell a product which offers the same outcomes as what your competitor's product offers unless you highlight your product's extra value. If your product doesn't add an extra feature, impact and corresponding value, it will not grab the customer's attention. Always do your homework before selling a product: study your competitor's products and look for any extra valuable outcome(s) that your product offers.

- **Change as a source of risk:**
  Customers always look at change as taking a risk. Remember, in every mind, the word change carries with it some associated risk factor. This also depends on the customer's personality; some customers are risk takers, and some are risk-averse.

  Your mission as a sales professional is to eliminate the risk factors and be prepared in advance to respond to any risks that the customer might think are present or possible. Risk factors are mainly related to the product's outcomes, efficacy, safety and patient satisfaction.
  Show the customer how the change will improve the current situation and will lead to better outcomes.

- **Patient outcomes:**
  An important factor that helps the customer make a buying decision is what the outcomes for patients/end users will be. Healthcare professionals (HCPs) are always trying to improve outcomes, and your presentation should focus on features, impacts, outcomes and values (examples will be given later).

- **Published product trials:**
  Among the sales aids which support selling are the published product trials and published articles found in medical journals. Customers value and respect these as evidence of product efficacy and safety. You must bring this kind of supportive evidence with you on your sales calls to help you close the deal effectively. Customers need to feel confident that the risks have been properly addressed and are no longer a barrier to proceeding.

- **Experience of other consumers/colleagues and testimonials:**
  People get influenced to buy when they see others buying the same product. It's a psychological element. They become comfortable when they see peers appreciate efficacy and safety. Make sure that your sales call includes such evidence. You can say 'this solution is clinically-proven and has helped 200,000 patients so far' and mention a study which supports that claim.

- **Company and sales representative's reputation:**
  Your company's reputation plays an important role in buying decisions. A reputation can be represented by its best customer service and ethics. Misrepresentation can happen from numerous causes: there is a delay in responding to customer requests; a sales representative fails to follow through on a customer's request; a product is unavailable when a physician prescribes it; misleading information is provided; a sales rep. doesn't follow the code of ethics or makes false claims; a sales rep. competes unfairly in the market place or belittles competitors.

- **Customer experience:**
  Past customer experiences with the company's products play an important role in the buying decision, and this experience is reflected onto every product that the company offers.

- **Quality of your sales call:**
  Your sales call quality and selling skills play a major role for buying decisions. If you built rapport, identified customer problems and challenges, uncovered the wishes/needs well, presented your product professionally, handled any objections

in a very satisfying manner and got a commitment from the customer, then the buying decision is guaranteed to be favorable.

- **'Chemistry' creation:**
  This an important factor to build relationships fast and improves your chances of sales call success. Chemistry is a simple "emotion" that two people get when they share a special connection. It is not necessarily sexual. It is the impulse making one think "I need to see this person again".

  Some people describe chemistry in metaphorical terms, such as 'like cookie dough and vanilla ice cream', or 'like a performance'. It can be described in terms of mutual feelings - "a connection, a bond or common feeling between two people".[5]

  Some of the core components of chemistry are: "similarity, attraction, mutual trust, and effortless communication."[6]

  Research and studies suggest that not everyone experiences chemistry. And that "chemistry occurred most often between people who are down-to-earth and sincere". This is because "if a person is comfortable with themselves, they are better able to express their true self to the world, which makes it easier to get to know them...even if perspectives on important matters differed." Sharing similarities is also deemed essential to chemistry as "feeling understood is essential to forming relational bonds".[7] (That's why we call it a support intervention).

- **Customer's emotional status:**
  If the customer doesn't seem to be in a good mood or looks upset, don't do the call. Instead, you can simply apologize and do it later.

Words to avoid using

If you were doing a presentation on a drug that was already approved by health authorities, and said, *"We have a new solution"*, your customer is going to think that your product isn't really approved yet, and it might still be in the trial stage.

When physicians hear the words 'new solution', they often think you're going to test the product on their patients and that it hasn't been tested enough to have proof of its efficacy and safety. This immediately translates into a risk factor that the physicians would want to avoid. You could instead say, *"Our company offers a great solution."* which sounds much better and doesn't trigger unnecessary fear of risk to patients.

Other wording that tends to raise red flags in your customer's mind is *"we don't recommend"*. This gives an impression of an opinion, which is not validated and supported and puts you at risk of rejection. It's better to say, "Based on the product trials, the product monograph recommends...", or you could say "The heart and stroke foundation recommends ...", or "The Center for Disease Control recommends ..." *Always cite* professional organizations whenever possible due to their credibility. Doing so sounds more professional and eliminates risk of rejection.

Other wording that can raise red flags is "We have *never heard this question before..."* or "This is the *first time we've ever had this question."* This gives an impression that your customer is asking a silly question and you will lose credibility. Instead, you could say something like '*"That's a great question."*

Saying that *"There are no side effects"* would be highly misleading because all drugs have side effects. You could simply say something like "This product has a very high safety profile" which is more realistic and more acceptable. If you do need to mention a side effect, you should mention the precaution related to the side effect.

Example: "Studies recommend taking the medication after meals, so patients can avoid stomach irritation."

Don't say: "Our product could cause stomach irritation."

Pay attention – watch – for the buying signals or signals to end conversation. Novice sales reps often miss the customer's signals that they're ready to make a commitment to their product. Be a great listener and observer. When the signals are present, stop presenting and close the deal.

Buying signals

Lot of sales professionals fail to pay attention to buying signals and keep talking when they should stop. Sometimes, they don't stop because they misread a buying signal as being an objection.

I was coaching a sales professional in a side visit when I was hired as a sales manager. While presenting the product, the customer said to the sales professional, "I am not quite sure about the concentration and if it's going to work in this specific indication".

The sales professional interpreted this sentence as an objection instead of a buying signal and responded to the customer with, "Why do you think it is not going to be effective?" among other questions. The customer became annoyed.

I picked up the conversation, and told the customer, "The best action to make sure that this concentration is effective is to try the product in this specific indication as indicated by the FDA approved trial. We would appreciate your feedback at our next visit. How many packs would you prefer initially to start the trial?" He asked us to leave 10 packs in the pharmacy and come back in two months. The trial worked perfectly, and the customer became one of our best prescribers.

My advice is to be a great listener and know when you should end your pitch and turn it into a close.

Some buying signals include:

- What about side effects?
- How much does it cost?
- How about precautions?
- Do you have some samples to try?
- How about the dose?
- How about safety?
- Is this product available in your warehouse?
- Which patients are the best candidates to use this?
- Could I use this for diabetic patients?
- Can you tell me more about this indication in detail?
- How about trials in cardiovascular patients?
- What have other physicians observed with this product?
- Repetition of features and their impacts.

When you hear any of these sentences, you must answer and close and move to your customer's commitment. There is no need to go on after that otherwise you will go back to square one and you might lose the sale.

2

Sales Call Objectives

First call on the product

In this type of call, there are many situations and scenarios. Either you launch a new product, or you re-launch an existing product. You need to determine if it's the first visit to the customer (a new customer) or if it's an existing customer on your list.

For the existing customer, there are two categories:

1. The customer may be someone who already prescribes, purchases, or uses your products or,
2. The customer has never prescribed or used (in a non-medical environment) any product from your company.

Every situation requires a different approach. For a first call to a new customer, your information about the customer is limited, so the best way to interact is to make sincere inquiries to better understand their prescribing behavior, and determine how they view your company services or products. Customers are usually very co-operative in this situation.

Dealing with customers who prescribe or use a competitor's product.

In this type of call, your research has revealed which products your customer uses or prescribes. There are different scenarios possible in this situation, so you need to know if the customer previously used or prescribed your product and then switched to a competitor's product.

This could have happened years earlier or could have happened recently. In this situation, you expect the switch happened because of an objection which was not resolved properly or there was an issue such as:

- side effects which the previous rep might not have addressed properly, or which could have been misrepresented by a competitor
- negative publication about your drug (product)or price
- lack of communication
- the release of a new drug (product) which has better outcomes and fewer or less significant side effects.

The most important point here is to focus on identifying the cause of the switch by asking your customer the reason and then addressing the concern.

Dealing with a customer who has never used your product or any other products except perhaps a competitor's product for many years

In this situation, your customer is probably firmly entrenched with the competitor. This is considered one of the most difficult situations you, as a sales rep, will face.

Based on our call success rate in this type of situation, we have concluded that the best technique to use is the same as what is used for indifferent personalities – the agreeable positive outcomes commitment (APOC) technique (see chapters 3 and 4).

Dealing with a customer who has tried products from various companies but has never tried your company's products.

This situation is likely due to lack of knowledge about your product due to:

- lack of customer visits, or
- your competitors are doing a good job, or
- negative publicity about your product.

You need to uncover your customer's *needs* and *wishes*.

Dealing with a customer who uses various products including yours.

If we delve more deeply into this situation, it appears that this customer likes to try different products and look for the best one in terms of efficacy and fewest side effects. This customer is usually a passive type, and (s)he accepts information without challenging it. So, you have a great opportunity to let the customer continue to use your product by making short but frequent visits to the customer and following the rules of the sales call from start to finish.

You need to do your research about the competitors and focus on your product's strengths.

Dealing with a customer who still hasn't prescribed or purchased your product even though you've already made the sales call to him or her.

You need to know if this situation happened with one customer, with a few of them or with a lot of customers. It's important that you do a post-call analysis and revise your plan following the steps detailed in this book.

If you apply what's written here, you will achieve a 99% success rate in your sales calls.

Follow-up calls for customers already using your product

In this sales call type, you need to do a plan for your sales call objective(s).

Reinforcement of prescribing behavior in the existing product indication.

Most sales reps try to get a commitment from their customers to pre-scribe a medication for all of the medication's indications, or in all groups of patients starting immediately. This can result in prescribing behavior failure. You might mention the full list of the medication's indications but when it comes to the commitment, take it one step at a time. In this type of call, you need to reinforce prescribing behavior for a specific indication that your customer is accustomed to prescribing. Later, in subsequent visits, after the physician has become comfortable prescribing that medication for one indication, the sales rep should seek a commitment from the physician to prescribe the medication for one of its other indications.

Same situation applies in non-medical sales, you need to reinforce the use of your product in a specific area of interest.

Expanding usage for different indications

In this type of call, once you are comfortable that your customer is pre-scribing your medication in one indication, then you can get the com-mitment to use it in another indication for the same group of patients (if your product has more than one indication for the same category of patients) in a separate visit.

An example of a non-medical sale is selling computer software services. If your customer uses a service you provide such as consulting and training, you could expand to include your services in programing and repairing. The key in expanding your services or product use is the customer satisfaction level in the existing service or use. In some sales situations, it would be beneficial to offer a bundle of services if you meet your customer for the first time, especially when you offer services.

Expanding usage in different categories of patients

For example, you have a product indicated to prevent or treat a type of blood clot called deep vein thrombosis (DVT), which can lead to blood clots in the lungs (pulmonary embolism). A DVT can occur after certain types of surgery, and it is also used in people with atrial fibrillation (a heart rhythm disorder) to lower the risk of stroke caused by a blood clot. If your customer is using the drug in the first group of patients, then you can expand usage into the second group of patients (the atrial fibrillation patients).

Expanding into a different specialty

The same anti-blood clot drug might be used in different specialties such as vascular surgery and cardiology.

In the medical devices industry, how the sales rep presents the product is often different to how the rep presents a prescribed product. In medical device sales presentations, all of the devices features and values are presented up front with the desired goal being that the customer will make a commitment to purchase the product soon.

If we assume that you have a cardiac output monitor that provides your customer with the hemodynamic parameters of a patient's heart using a pulmonary artery wedge pressure catheter, you can't focus on one visit for anesthesia on the use of the machine to determine the continuous cardiac output and in another visit on different indications which could be used to determine systemic vascular resistance or in another visit for stroke volume and stroke volume variation. In this example, the anesthesiologist wants to see all parameters on the same screen, so you can't mention just one indication in each visit. You have to mention all of them in one visit and mention the corresponding impact of having each parameter on the monitor screen because all of those parameters form an important group of information to monitor heart function.

However, you could expand the use of the machine in different departments such as emergency, ICU, and CCU.

So, setting your call objective is crucial for your call to be a success. *You need to determine:*

- who your target customer is,
- what you are going to present, and,
- what the important topics to discuss are.
- Always put yourself in your customer's position and identify your call objective and build your presentation based on that objective.

Ideally, your objective should:

- target a specific area for improvement,
- suggest an indicator of progress,
- specify who will do it,
- state what results can realistically be achieved given the available resources, and,
- specify when the result(s) can be achieved and evaluated.

Now you are well-prepared, having gathered info about your customer, identified your call type, and know which product you are calling on. Now it's time to prepare for your call opening.

3
The APWS Selling Method

The APWS Selling Model can be applied not only for healthcare product sales but for sales of almost any type of product in any industry.

A = Awareness.
Increase awareness about a common, existing problem.

The main goal is to let the customer know and become consciously aware of a common existing problem in a specific population of patients across different clinical practices and relate to the customer how your solution helped other practitioners with similar patient populations meet their patients' medical needs. The point here is to let your customers feel that they are not facing the problem alone but that their colleagues also encounter this problem. You should make your customers feel that your solution will solve the problem for them just as it has helped their colleagues working elsewhere solve theirs. This creates a comfort level and biases your customer in favor of believing and trusting what you will subsequently be saying about your solution.

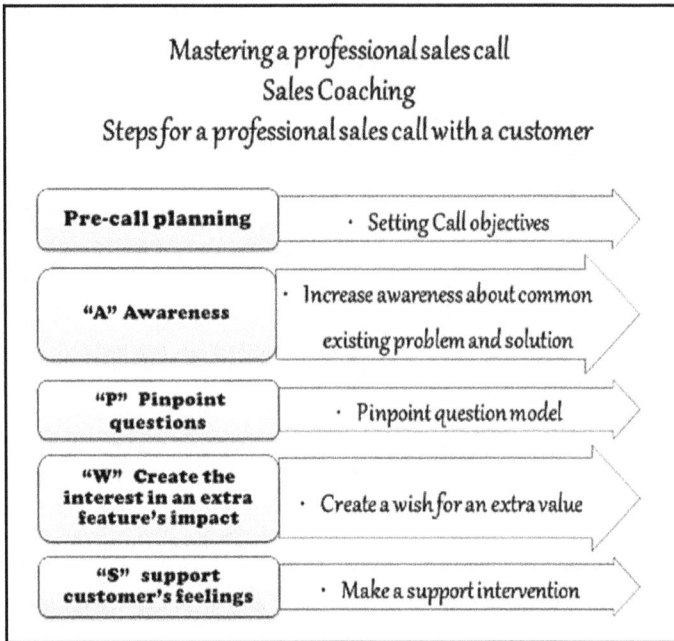

Mastering a professional sales call
Sales Coaching
Steps for a professional sales call with a customer

Pre-call planning	· Setting Call objectives
"A" Awareness	· Increase awareness about common existing problem and solution
"P" Pinpoint questions	· Pinpoint question model
"W" Create the interest in an extra feature's impact	· Create a wish for an extra value
"S" support customer's feelings	· Make a support intervention

Example:

SELLER: (*Awareness statement*) "This great solution has helped 150,000 patients so far who were suffering from menopause symptoms like hot flashes, sweats, and pain during intercourse. Most of the physicians were happy to see their patients get relief and be able to enjoy their normal daily life activities again."

P = Pinpoint.

Ask pinpoint questions to obtain key information

Definition of Pinpoint questions:

"Pinpoint questions lead your customer to better understand the problem and to be focused on the proposed solution for a problem."

The questions you ask your customer are very important. It's a crucial step for your sales call success and must be mastered. Questions need to be specific. Based on your customer's responses you will be able to identify what your customer's needs and wishes are.

To ask pinpoint questions, you need to know the types of questions you should ask. There are eight types of questions:

- Need-identifying questions,
- Product-outcome gap identifying questions,
- Wish-creating questions,
- Problem-identifying questions,
- Problem's outcomes-identifying questions,
- Solution-Input questions,
- Commitment-leading questions, and,
- Agreeable Positive Outcome questions.

Need-identifying questions.

Questions usually asked to stimulate a customer's interest in a new solution which hasn't been implemented in the customer's practice.

You ask these questions if your customer isn't using a product that is identical to yours or if your customer isn't using a similar product presently or your product has a totally different mechanism of action. In this last case you need to create or identify the needs for your new (product) solution. These questions should relate your new solution to your product's impacts and outcomes.

Example:

> SELLER: *(Need-identifying question)* "What are the most important criteria you are looking for in a drug controlling weight loss?"

Product-outcome gap identifying questions

These are among the most important questions you will encounter when you face a sales situation in which your customer is using a direct competitor. These questions usually focus on identifying the outcome/value gap for the existing competing product in use, which results when the existing product in use lacks a meaningful value compared with what you can offer the customer with your product. In most sales situations, customers don't realize that the existing product in use is missing a significant value, and it's the sales professional's responsibility to direct her/his customer's attention to that significant value difference.

> SELLER: *(product-outcome gap identifying question)*
> "You mentioned that the existing camera surveillance would be able to monitor an area across a 90-degree radius. What if you wanted to monitor the area across 180 degrees or more?" (the seller offers a camera that provides 360-degree surveillance)
>
> CUSTOMER: "Well, we wouldn't be able to see more than 90 degrees."
>
> SELLER: "That means that the existing 90-degree surveillance camera gives you only 25% of the surveillance performance that a 360-degree surveillance camera would, and any security breach could happen in the 75% of the image that your existing camera can't capture. Is that correct?"
>
> CUSTOMER: That's correct.

The seller was successful in identifying the existing product outcome/value gap and would be able to fill in the gap by offering a wide-range camera surveillance system that would give better security.

Wish-creating questions.

These questions usually focus on identifying an extra valued feature's impact and its outcomes relative to what the competitor offers. These questions are used if the customer is using a similar product or a product that has a similar mechanism of action. These questions are based on initiating the interest for an extra feature's impacts and pointing out why your product is superior. The goal is to emphasize the superior outcomes of your product and how they enhance your product's value.

It would be easy to confuse the *need* with the *wish* here, but remember in this situation, from the customer's point of view, the *need* already exists if he or she is using a similar product and you must highlight the extra valued feature provided by your product. That's why it's crucial to ask questions to let the customer identify his/her wishes by having an extra value compared to the current product in use.

In the previous example:

> SELLER: *(Wish-creating question)* "How do you see the value of using a surveillance camera which would provide you full 360 degree surveillance so you would be able to

monitor 100% of the image and avoid any security breach compared to the limited range offered by a 90-degree surveillance camera?"

Another examples:

SELLER: *(Wish-creating question)* "What specific differences in the product are you looking for that would improve your patient's outcomes?"

SELLER: *(Wish-creating question)* "What kind of difference are your patients looking for compared with what they are using right now?"

SELLER: *(Wish-creating question)* "What kind of an added features, impacts or outcomes would you like to have compared to what the current medication is capable of offering?"

SELLER: *(Wish-creating question)* "I am quite confident that your patients would appreciate much better outcomes. What would you think the current product is missing in terms of safety and efficacy?"

You might wonder: What if the customer mentions a feature's outcome which can't be provided by your product?

That means that you haven't built a professional attention grabber. Remember that you must build your attention grabber before asking the pin-point questions which lead your customer's focus to be on the proposed solution for a problem. Your questions need to be focused on how to solve the problem you have mentioned in the attention grabber.

Example:

SITUATION: From your research about your competitor, you discovered that the competitor's product is causing stomach irritation while your product doesn't irritate stomachs.

SELLER: (APOC question) "Would your patients prefer a drug which doesn't cause stomach irritation?"

CUSTOMER: Sure!

In this situation you are creating the customer's desire to have the wish by having an extra feature's impact and value.

Problem-identifying questions.

These are questions that identify the causes of an existing problem such as when you discover that your customer experienced a problem with your product, or your customer called you to consult about a solution to a problem. You need to identify the cause of the problem, analyze it, find the best options and offer the best solutions that satisfy your customer's *needs* or *wishes*.

<u>Example:</u>

> SELLER: "I would like to have details about it."
>
> SELLER: "Would you please tell me more about this?"
>
> SELLER: "In your experience, what do you believe is the main cause of this issue?"
>
> SELLER: "How did this issue start and how did you deal with it?"
>
> SELLER: "Does it happen with all of your patients?"
>
> SELLER: "Why do you think this happened?"

Note that the sales rep. never utters the word 'problem'.

Problem's outcomes-identifying questions

These are some of the most important questions in your sales call. Problem outcomes happen when the problem's impacts persist unresolved for a period of time. These questions help your customer understand the problem as well as the consequences of letting the problem persist. Customers realize that it's necessary to make a change as soon as possible.

Example based on an actual situation:

> SELLER: "From what has been discussed, you mentioned that your surgical instruments are coming out 80% clean *(Problem)*. How does this impact the cost of the re-cleaning cycle?)" *(Increase awareness about the problem's impact)*
>
> BUYER: *(Problem's impact)* "It adds about $100 to the cost of each cleaning cycle."

SELLER: "How many re-cleaning cycles are you running per day?"

BUYER: "Three cycles."

SELLER: *(Problem's outcome)* "Let me see what it's costing you then to have to re-clean instruments over the course of six months. It comes to $53000." *(severe problem's outcome over time)*

BUYER: "I didn't realize that we pay that much." *(great recognition developing for the problem's outcomes)*

Solution-Input questions

These are questions asked immediately after you ask the problem outcome's identifying questions. It's your solution that will prevent the undesirable consequences of an existing problem's outcome.

In the Previous example:

SELLER: "How does that sound if we offered much better outcomes from the first cleaning cycle and avoid the costs incurred from re-cleaning?" *(Solution-input question)*

BUYER: "That would be amazing." *(Customer compelled to make an urgent change)*

Commitment-leading questions.

These are questions posed mainly toward the end of your sales call which ask for a commitment from your customer. The best way to ask for a commitment is to ask a question which leads the customer to take the following actions in his/her mind:

1. Think and analyze.
2. Recap the features and impacts/outcomes/values in mind.
3. Decide.
4. Act.

Just before asking these sorts of questions, you should summarize the features and impacts which the customer has already accepted as being true/valid and to help your customer to recap them to him- or herself.

Example:

> SELLER: *(Strong commitment leading question)* "We just summarized *(name of your product)*. Would you please give me an example of the type of patient who would best benefit by using *(your product's name)*?"

Agreeable Positive Outcomes (APOC) questions

These questions are best used with customers who appear to be indifferent to your products or who are firmly entrenched using a competitor's products. Such customers tend to be quiet and unengaged during your sales call. The sales rep should ask questions which lead the customer to acknowledge and agree about the positive outcomes provided by your product.

For example

> SELLER: *(APOC question)* "How does it sound if we offer a solution to reduce blood pressure with the fewest side effects and highest efficacy? Would this be much better for your patient outcomes?"
>
> CUSTOMER: "Definitely, we always look for better outcomes!"

Another example:

> SELLER: *(APOC question)* "How does it sound if we offer a debugging computer software that adds speed-boosting, privacy protection, real-time optimization, deep registry cleaning and 24/7 technical support with no extra cost, would this be more convenient for use and cost savings?
>
> CUSTOMER: "Sure."

The goal here is to let your customer engage and agree about positive outcomes, which is a signal to you that you will successfully close the deal. This technique will be explained in detail below.

W = Wish.

Wish creation.

Create a customer's desire to have an extra valued impact that results in superior outcomes and values.

There is a difference between satisfying the need and satisfying the wish. To better understand the difference, you need to know the exact definition for each.

Sometimes customers simply don't know that they could be getting a better solution than what they've settled with up until now and the sales professional should point out to customers that they really should be wishing for better outcomes. A *wish* in this context refers to instilling in the customer a desire to have an extra valued feature along with its related positive impacts. This ultimately rewards the patient/healthcare facility due to superior outcomes compared with what the customer had been using or prescribing. For example, a physician needs a drug to reduce blood pressure, but (s)he could wish this drug would offer the fewest side effects yet provide the highest efficacy. In most of the cases, the *wish* will be dormant or unrecognized by the customer. Sometimes customers know their *wishes* but never mention them. It is the sales rep's job to create the customer's desire for an extra value.

Most sales reps find it difficult to get a customer to switch from using a competing product to one of the sales rep's products. In most cases, when a customer knows that the sales reps are offering a similar product, they refuse to meet with the sales rep. The difference is explained in detail later.

Fulfilling a *wish* may cost more money than fulfilling a *need* because of the extra feature's impact and outcomes.

When customers are already using a competitor's product, it is essential that you create the *wish* and to do so, you must focus on your product's extra-valued features and their related impact compared to those of the competing product.

S = Support Intervention.

Essentials for sales call success:

Chemistry in customer relationships is an important component to sales call success. Some people might argue that good 'chemistry' is not essential for successful sales calls. But, we must ask ourselves if the outcomes would be the same if we have didn't have good chemistry with a customer. Well, you know the answer to that.

Chemistry is directly related to building rapport. Without chemistry no rapport can be created. The combination of good chemistry and rapport makes the sales rep and the customer feel engaged and pleased to be in the presence of each other.

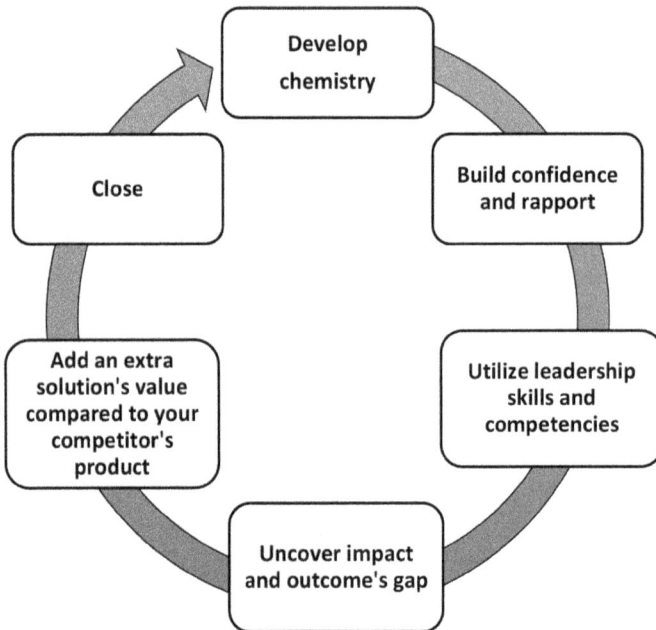

There is a debate over whether chemistry can be artificially developed if it is not initially present.

Support intervention is the first step in developing chemistry. In this stage, you, the sales rep, intervene to support your customer's opinion. It occurs right after asking probing questions to uncover the customer's problems, needs or wishes and then waiting for your customer's responses to those questions. Your support intervention consists of supporting what the customer said.

> SELLER: "What is most important to you about a car insurance policy?"
>
> CUSTOMER: "I care about the two-way coverage and the cost of the premium."
>
> SELLER: "Yes, I definitely agree. You've identified the most important points which I am going to talk about." (This is a support intervention sentence.)

Another example:

> SELLER: "How would you describe our customer support so far?"
>
> CUSTOMER: "I am not highly satisfied."
>
> SELLER: "Sorry to hear that. Would you please tell me more about this? I am here to provide support. (Another support intervention statement)
>
> CUSTOMER: "I requested some samples a while ago and they took long time to arrive."
>
> SELLER: "That's not convenient at all. Would you allow me the time to look into it and see what happened to make sure that this situation will never happen again?" (A support intervention statement)

The sales professional's facial expressions should reflect the seriousness of the matter, as a part of tactical empathy. The sales professional should feel and share his customer's emotions and thoughts. It's tactical or strategic empathy to achieve a desired end.

The relationship between problems, needs and wishes

It's important to identify customer problems first and then ask questions which lead customers to mention their *wishes* to solve these problems by recognizing a value and its impact on the patient/the customer's daily practice.

Everyone wishes for solutions to their problems. For example, a person could wish for 18-inch wheels on her/his car for greater stability and safety on the road. What is the problem initially? That the customer has a car which was not stable on the road, which could not offer enough safety for her/his family. Does wishing your car had 18-inch wheels constitute a need or a wish?

If the customer has the budget to change the wheels, then they could be changed. If (s)he doesn't have the budget, then he will use the same wheels until he can pay for bigger ones. In this case, changing wheels is not a need because he has a car already, but he wishes to have 18-inch wheels on it. Then it's a wish he dreams about to be safer on the road. Is it an important wish? Yes, of course.

Another example:

A physician prescribes an anti-hypertensive drug which has side effects, and you are a sales rep presenting the physician with info about a new anti-hypertensive drug with lower side effects. Would you be, in this case, looking after the customer's need for a new anti-hypertensive drug or do you need to create the wish to have an extra feature's impact and outcome that are superior to what your customer has been prescribing? Is this a wish creation or a need creation?

To answer this question, you must think, that if the physician learned of a drug with fewer side effects and significant efficacy, then the physician would prescribe it. If the physician couldn't find a drug with fewer side effects, then (s)he will continue to prescribe the existing medication.

What exactly is the physician looking for? Certainly not just another anti-hypertensive drug. The physician is looking for an extra-valued outcome, which represents extra valued features, impacts and outcomes.

That's a common selling mistake that happens when a sales professional's focus is on selling a product that is similar to a competing product that a customer is already using. Instead, the sales professional must focus on creating the customer's desire or bond with an extra valued feature. Again, it's a wish and it has to be created. The need for blood-pressure lowering drugs is already present, but the physician wishes there was a drug with fewer side effects that would therefore be safer for the patient. Is this an important wish? Yes, certainly.

Example:

If the physician uses a beta blocker to reduce blood pressure, it might have side effects including fatigue, dizziness and weakness. The sales professional offers a similar product like an ACE inhibitor to reduce blood pressure. Your focus should be on creating an extra feature's impact and outcome which shows your product's superiority over beta blockers, and facilitates a return to normal life activities for the patient, such as driving, normal mental focus (which leads to excellent work performance daily), and no dizziness or fatigue.

The focus here is not to create the need for a new anti-hypertensive (ACE inhibitor) but to create the wish among prescribing physicians to restore to their patients the ability to engage in normal daily life activities without the fear of serious effects or increased risks, such as driving while not being at their best.

What is the definition of the Wish in a sales situation?

A wish is created when a customer learns from you about the impact and the related outcomes that your product offers that the customer's present product doesn't offer. Your product's extra features have an impact and one or more related outcomes to your customer's work practices that the customer was previously unaware of and now wishes to have implemented, and, or your product resolves the problem that your customer is routinely having to work around using his or her present product, and would be saved time/money/hassles if another product or process would eliminate the need for the work-around. It is the job of the sales professional to identify the shortcomings of the customer's present workplace/clinical practices that are causing the customer extra work, higher costs, higher risk, damage to other equipment – whatever the case may be in each work environment – and to shape the customer's thinking until the customer realizes he or she can successfully address existing workplace challenges (improve safety, save staff time, pay lower maintenance or equipment costs, etc.) by seeking the solution you are offering.

Customers may know what they wish were available in a product, or they may not have thought about it. It is the APWS sales person's job to help the customer develop a wish for a better solution. To do this, the sales professional must see what the customer might not be able to see. For example, if the sales professional has a solution that saves the customer time or money, or saves the customer from high product maintenance costs, then it's up to the sales professional to identify the impact, value, and outcome that the customer would appreciate, and plant the seed in the customer's mind that the new solution is superior for the customer or the particulars of the workplace practices. Remember, the customer may not be aware of or have time to really consider how his current product falls short (existing product-outcome gap), or how a change in product could reap multiple rewards in terms of cost, reduced hazards, greater enjoyment, ease of use, superior performance, durability, reduced maintenance or storage costs, improved safety for staff, etc.

What is the difference between satisfying the Need and satisfying the Wish?

In the past, we have learned from many books and trainers about looking for the needs and satisfying the need by mentioning the features and benefits. We can't call every situation a need. If a customer is using a product and you are offering a similar product, in this situation and from a customer's point of view there is no actual need to change products.

If you are trying to sell a car to someone who doesn't have a car because she is late in arriving at work every day using public transit, if she walked in a show room to buy a car, is she trying to fulfill a need or a wish? A need, because the customer needs a car to move easily from one place to another and to arrive on time. Does an extra valued feature's impact and outcome play a role here? Not really, because we sell for the need and not for the wish in this case. So the car salesperson who tries to sell an extra feature and impact which happens to increase the price of the car will be wasting his time because the customer doesn't need or value that feature.

If the customer has a 2015 car and wants to have the most recent model instead, that is a *wish* because the need is already met by having a car in the first place. In this case the customer wishes to have a car with extra-valued features and impacts (new safety features, heated seats for winter, GPS, etc..), so in this case the salesperson should focus on extra-valued features rather than just trying to sell him or her a simple replacement for his 2015 car.

As another example, a car salesperson in a show room is selling a new car to a pregnant woman who has one child and a car built in 2006. The salesperson saw the lady staring at a nice car in the show room, so he approached her and started to mention the following:

> SELLER: This car reaches 100km per hour in just 6 seconds.
> SELLER: It has a turbo engine, so it will be very smooth to drive.
> SELLER: It has 6 speed gear with automatic transmission, so you'll get great speed on the highway.

Is she is going to buy the car? Big NO. She will run away from the showroom.

The seller was trying to sell a car with high speed which is not really important for that customer. That particular customer wasn't looking for a fast car, since she would not want to risk her child and her pregnancy. The salesperson didn't mention any extra-valued features and outcomes that mattered to that customer. He focused on the speedy engine which might be a wish for some other drivers, but not this particular customer. She needed a car and wishes for a car that has extra safety features (wishes always would cost more money). Instead of assuming the lady valued the same things as the salesperson valued, the salesperson should have uncovered the customer's wishes first and then provided the information about the product that would have satisfied her wishes for a very safe car.

Selling to the Wish

Another salesperson in the same show room trying to sell the same lady the same car mentions the following:

> SELLER: Do you have a car right now?
> CUSTOMER: Yes, I have a 2006 Honda.
> SELLER: *(A wish-creating question)* What kind of things would you like your next car to offer? Remember that in wish-creation questions, you are comparing what you offer with the competing product in use, and that is to create an extra value.
> CUSTOMER: To be more comfortable and to be safer than what I presently have in my old car.
> SELLER: *(Support intervention statement)* You exactly nailed it about the most important features in this car.

SELLER: This car is different from what you have. It has an excellent safety lock system *(Feature)* which is activated once you start the engine. It prevents kids from opening doors accidently *(Impact)* while you're driving so there is better safety for them *(Value)*.

SELLER: When you ride and drive, you will feel a unique shock absorber system *(Feature)*. You won't feel any bumps in the road *(Impact)* so you and your passengers will be more comfortable *(Outcome)* and safer *(Value)*.

SELLER: This car is built with side-impact bars made of steel *(Feature)*, so if a car hits you on the side, the cabin won't be affected *(Impact)* and will be safer *(Value)*.

SELLER: This car has an added 10 air bags inside the cabin, so all passengers are fully protected.

Is she is going to buy? **Likely, yes.**

Is this salesperson selling to the need or the wish? He focused on a car with extra-valued features and outcomes that were absent in the car that the customer owned, thus he is selling to the wish.

The first salesperson focused on an existing need of having a car, but he didn't mention any valued impacts and outcomes.

The second salesperson satisfied the customer's wishes by identifying the car's features that fulfilled her wishes.

What is the difference between Needs and Wants?

If a customer said he wanted a red car, but there was no red car available, would the salesperson be able to sell the customer another color? Yes, if the red car is not available, then the salesperson could convince the customer to pick another great color. Buying decisions are adversely affected when needs are not met, but not when wants are not met.

Another example:

If a customer wants to buy a pack of cigarettes and the package has a disgusting picture on the outside, and the customer asks the salesclerk to get him a different pack of cigarettes because he doesn't like the picture on the first package, if the salesclerk doesn't have a pack with a less disgusting picture and in fact all the packs have the same picture on them, will the customer buy cigarettes or not? There is a 90% chance that the customer will buy a pack because the customer needs the cigarettes.

Wants do not negatively impact buying decisions compared to *wishes* or *needs*, however if you as the sales person could find a pack of cigarettes that didn't have the unappetizing picture on it, the customer would be especially happy about the purchase.

Transferring the Wish into an urgent request in complex or large sales

It's important to let the customer realize his wishes to solve a problem. Problems arise when an existing product lacks a meaningful value. The problem or issue could be dormant or neglected by the customer for several reasons:

- **Customer's problem-bond**
  The customer is accustomed to the problem and has become bonded to it, a situation which we call a customer problem bond.
- **Lack of information provided**
  The customer doesn't want to change the procedure or the product on the assumption that it is still easier for him or her to use the current product. In this specific situation, the sales professional mentioned the outcomes and values of his/ her new solution but never mentioned how to implement the solution in the practice, or how much more easily and efficiently the staff could use the new product compared to the product they've been using. It is important for sales pro-fessionals not to leave it to their customers to take a guess at how to use new products. Otherwise, there is considerable risk that customers would presume that it's easier to keep using what they've been using, and they'll never change products.
- **Administrative hassle**
  The customer doesn't want to change products or procedures because there would be a lot of administrative hassle involved.

If you have been successful in showing the customers how they would gain by implementing your new solution, then customers are willing to endure that administrative hassle. Always offer support during the conversion or change process and ask the customer: What kind of support would you like from me to facilitate the conversion or change process? There could be multiple decision-makers involved in approving a change in product selection. This is most likely happening for every product change within the facility, which is why it's crucial to meet with every decision maker in your initial contact so as to secure their approval.

- **Inventory Status**

  The customer wants to change but he still has a lot of inventory on hand from the existing product. In this situation you would either ask for a purchase order with post-dated scheduled delivery based on the customer's preference, once their inventory is depleted, or, if his inventory is not large, you could offer to buy the remaining inventory and apply a credit note to your first invoice to the customer. Don't leave getting your purchase order to chance, always offer solutions in order to secure your P.O.

- **Existing product -outcome gap**

  The customer was not aware of the problem until somebody pointed it out. This is a common situation you will face on a daily basis. Even if you mastered the probing questions professionally, most of the customers don't really know that they have a problem or an issue. Very often, customers will say they're satisfied using a competing product, when in fact that product might lack a meaningful value. That's why we call it a product-outcome gap relative to what your product could do. Your mission is first to identify the existing gap and then fill in the gap by identifying those aspects of your product that are lacking in the competing product (using the wish creation technique). To know what's missing in the competing product, you need to have your customer's permission to stay in their department to observe how it's performing for the customer/facility. Ideally, if you can get the department manager to walk you through the process, that would be great, because then you can identify all the outcome gaps. If this is not possible, then you need to know what your customer is currently using, and then you will know what the gaps are.

A major client of mine in Ontario called me because her staff members were experiencing allergies and skin eczema, and they wanted to try our hand sanitizer to see if they would get relief from those problems. Immediately I recognized what the gap is with current product. I knew what they were using and what kind of outcome gap existed because the competing product didn't have enough emollients in it. In addition, I found that this major account was using a hand soap and hand lotion from the same competing company, and there were two more outcome gaps for each one of those products. Their hand soap contained a harsh ingredient for the skin, and the hand lotion didn't have Panthenol (a skin builder). The customer thought that the problem was only being caused by the hand sanitizer but hadn't considered the impact of the other two substances, simply due to a lack of awareness about it. In the end, the customer elected to buy our three products instead of just buying one product.

- The customer wanted to make changes but hadn't found a better solution.

The process should be initiated by you, the sales professional, who identifies an existing problem that a competitor's product hasn't solved but is in use in the customer's practice (e.g., the competitor's product lacks your product's significant impact or great value), and increases awareness that your solution has this missing value. You further point out that your solution is in common use by various customers. Once the problem is identified, then you start creating *wishes* (in cases in which the customer is using a competitor's product). Once the wishes are created then you must relate *wishes* for solving the problem to a product's impact and extra value which then convert a customer's *wishes* into a reality. Once the customer realizes the product's extra feature's impact to solve the problem, then *wishes* will become a request to be resolved.

To summarize, you should look for your product's extra feature's impact, outcome and value and compare them to what the competitor's product offers, and thus identify the extra value that the customer would enjoy.

Transforming the need into an urgent request

As mentioned before, a customer's *need* can be generated if the customer doesn't have a product or a solution for an existing issue in his daily practice. If, for example, you are offering a product that has no competing product, or, there might be a competing product but it uses a totally different mechanism, if the competing product partially solves a customer's problem, then it's important to create a need for your new solution.

In this case it's not called a *wish* because the *wish* (as mentioned before), is developing desire and a bond between the customer and an extra feature's impact and outcome compared to an existing product's performance in the facility.

In this situation, you don't need to look for *wishes* but you must look first for a problem's impact and related severe outcomes on the customer's practice and create a *need* for a solution related to your product.

In the past, there was no differentiation between the *needs* and the *wishes*. Sales professionals were always looking for the *needs* in all situations. Even on occasions when the customer was using a competitor's product, they were trying to create a *need* for it, which is why in most of the cases they experienced failure and got a lot of rejections.

Let's look at the following example to explain the difference:

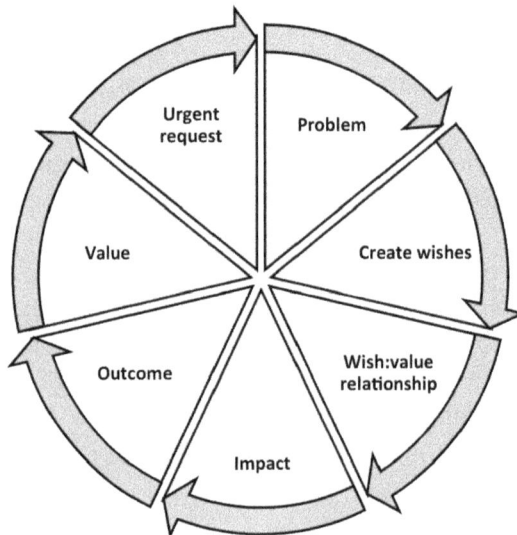

Wish creation

Scenario:

You are presenting a detergent to clean surgical instruments and the detergent you are offering has three enzymes: protease, amylase, and lipase.

Your customer uses a detergent which has only two enzymes: protease and amylase. You determined during the uncover stage that some instruments are coming out of the cleaning process only 80% clean (example of a product that has a problem-outcome gap), particularly the instruments used in orthopedic surgeries. Your customer doesn't know why this happened although they were using their detergent which utilizes only two enzymes. You must create the wish of having the third enzyme which is lipase because lipids are the predominant soiling factor in orthopedic surgeries making the instruments greasier and harder to clean.

WHEN YOU SELL TO A CUSTOMER WHO IS USING A COMPETITOR'S PRODUCT, TRY TO IDENTIFY A PRODUCT'S OUTCOME/VALUE GAP

In this case your customer uses a competing product that uses almost the same mechanism using enzyme technology but it's missing a huge impact, outcome and corresponding value, which is an important enzyme (lipase) that dissolves lipids and ensures the orthopedic instruments are 100% clean.

Your mission is to show the value for an extra feature/impact/ outcome by having your lipase enzyme added to the existing two, 100% efficient product instead of the competitor's two-enzyme, 80% efficient product, and let the customer develop a *wish* to have lipase added. The *wish* always costs more money.

You might say, why we don't call this situation a *need*? Simply because you are offering the same technology and the customer doesn't really need an enzymatic detergent, because (s)he already has one.

The questions you need to ask in order to create the *wish* are different from the questions you need to ask to create the *need*. Refer to the Pinpoint question model.

Questions to create the Wish:

SELLER: "Given what you have told me, how do you deal with the instruments coming out only 80% clean?"

CUSTOMER: "That's our challenge. We need to re-clean the instruments every time."

SELLER: "I agree, it's a big challenge (Support intervention). I believe that in the re-cleaning process, you need to manually clean the instruments first and then re-do a cleaning cycle. Is that correct?"

CUSTOMER: "Yes, correct."

SELLER: *(creating the wish for reducing cost)* "How does this impact your cleaning and labor costs?"

CUSTOMER: "They are very high."

SELLER: *(Problem outcome-identifying questions)* "I believe that you have another challenge if we consider the added consequences of having to re-clean, and what that costs over time. When did this problem first occur?" *(the problem's consequences over time triggers the customer to ask for an urgent change)*

CUSTOMER: "It started two years ago." *(customer should now realize the long-term effect of the problem's consequences going unaddressed)* "

SELLER: *(Creating the wish of adding lipase)* "Orthopedic instruments are usually soiled with lipids which are hard to clean. How do you find the final cleaning performance for orthopedic instruments using protease and amylase only *(put emphasis on the word only)* in a double enzymatic detergent?"

CUSTOMER: "Our instruments are coming out only 90% clean in the final process. Do we need to add something extra?"

SELLER: *(Presentation model using FIOV)* "Definitely. *(Feature)* Adding lipase to a double enzymatic detergent ensures *(Impact)* 100% cleaning performance from the first cleaning cycle by dissolving the lipids on the orthopedic instruments and *(Outcome)* fully maximizes the cleaning from bioburden and avoids *(Value)* costs resulting from re-cleaning the instruments."

CUSTOMER: "We would love to do a trial if you have some available." *(The wish transferred to an urgent request to be implemented)*

Explanation for the pinpoint question (wish creating question):

The sales professional here asked questions which compared what he offers with what the customer is currently using, mentioning the ingredients followed by the word 'only'. The word 'only' is a hint directed at the customer to point out that there must be an additional ingredient that needs to be added to make the detergent more effective at cleaning. The sales professional succeeded in paying his customer attention to the problem's added consequences over time (Problem's outcome), which triggered the customer for doing a trial, immediate product change and eventually securing the P.O.

The sales rep., in creating the *wish* focused on the extra feature's impact, outcome and value compared to what the customer was using. The sales rep in this case succeeded in identifying the gap between what they are using and the new solution. Remember the definition of the *wish*: Developing a customer's desire and a bond creation between the customer and an extra feature's impact and outcome compared with what the customer is currently using.

Q to create the need (if the rep were trying to create the need):

SELLER: "Orthopedic instruments are usually soiled with lipids which are hard to clean, necessitating a need for a triple enzymatic detergent."

CUSTOMER: "It's okay, we are okay."

SELLER: "Yes, I understand, and triple enzymatic detergent has lipase which is essential for orthopedic instrument cleaning."

CUSTOMER: "We don't have the budget right now to change to a new one." (This is an excuse to end the discussion.)

Did the sales rep. let the customer know what her problem's impacts and related outcomes are? No, Did the sales rep. focus her/his customer's attention on the problem's added consequences over time? No, Did the sales rep. here focus on an extra feature's impact and outcome compared with what the customer is presently using? No, the sales rep. focused on selling another enzymatic detergent. The sales rep. focused on initiating interest about a solution which already exists in the customer's practice or a solution which is similar to what the customer has, which led to failure of the sale.

The customer heard 'enzymatic detergent' and immediately noted that (s)he already has one on hand, so there was no need to change products and the customer failed to discern the value of the word 'triple'. If the sales rep. had later tried to convince the customer of the importance of lipase in the detergent, there is a 90% probability that his efforts would have failed because it is very hard to change a customer's mind after the customer has initially given any consideration to the proposed product.

In creating the *wish*, once the customer realizes the value behind lipase and the problem added consequences over time, then the *wish* will immediately be transformed into an urgent request to buy the triple enzymatic detergent.

Need creation

Scenario:

Let's use the same example as above: you are offering a triple enzymatic detergent. Your customer is using a detergent that doesn't have enzymes at all, such as sodium hydroxide, which only renders instruments 60% clean. The customer doesn't know why they aren't 100% clean.

In this case it's not a *wish* creation because the customer is using a totally different product that employs a totally different mechanism of action.

The customer is not aware of the importance of enzymes in the cleaning process, although (s)he is using a detergent, but your product is considered a new cleaning protocol to be implemented.

You should focus on creating the *need* for a totally new solution involving a product that uses enzymes in the cleaning process. This customer doesn't need an extra feature and impact compared with their existing product, because the customer doesn't have a similar product. You might wonder why we don't call this situation a *wish* creation. Well, it's simply because you cannot add an extra value to sodium hydroxide. Actually, sodium hydroxide should be replaced by triple enzymatic detergent, although in the example of *wish* creation the double enzymatic detergent should be replaced too by a triple enzymatic detergent, but the customer gets sold on the extra valued feature's impact and outcome compared to the customer's similar product.

Once your customer realizes how important it is to use enzymes to clean, the customer will develop an urgent need to buy your triple enzymatic detergent.

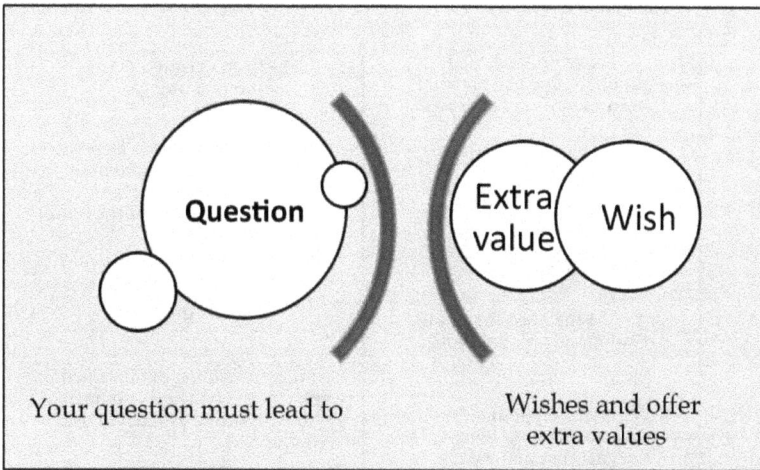

| Question | Extra value | Wish |

Your question must lead to   Wishes and offer extra values

Let's recap:

Dealing with Customers using a competitor in steps:

1. Existing product-outcome gap(s):

Most of the problems in the customer's practice, especially those who are using a direct competitor's product, arise when the competing product in use lacks a meaningful value or it has shortcomings.

These gaps result in an ongoing problem due to its added consequences over time which can cause harm and perhaps severely damage the customer's practice or the end users.

Your first step dealing with those customers is to identify the shortcomings or what we call the existing product-outcome gap of the existing product in use that your product would overcome.

Once you identify the existing product-outcome gaps, then you need to focus your customer's attention on those gaps by asking the following pinpoint questions:

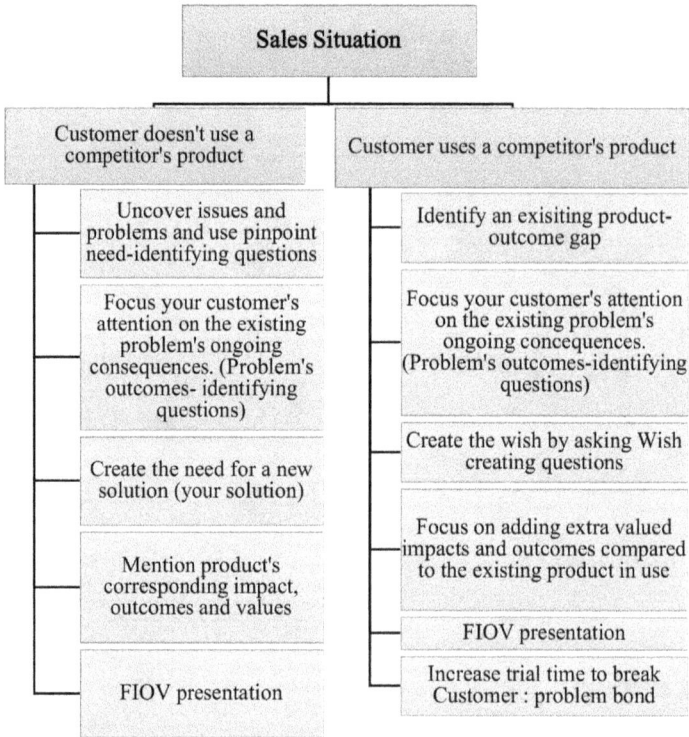

```
                        ┌─────────────────────┐
                        │   Sales Situation   │
                        └─────────────────────┘
```

Customer doesn't use a competitor's product	Customer uses a competitor's product
Uncover issues and problems and use pinpoint need-identifying questions	Identify an exisiting product-outcome gap
Focus your customer's attention on the existing problem's ongoing consequences. (Problem's outcomes- identifying questions)	Focus your customer's attention on the existing problem's ongoing concequences. (Problem's outcomes-identifying questions)
Create the need for a new solution (your solution)	Create the wish by asking Wish creating questions
Mention product's corresponding impact, outcomes and values	Focus on adding extra valued impacts and outcomes compared to the existing product in use
	FIOV presentation
FIOV presentation	Increase trial time to break Customer : problem bond

2. Product outcome/value gap-identifying questions:
This is the second step following identifying the existing product gaps. Asking these questions will let your customer realize the main problem and where it comes from. Examples were provided.

3. Problem outcome-identifying questions:
What is the problem's outcome: It's the potential adverse effects resulting from a problem's impact going unresolved over the course of weeks, months, or even years, and which can result in significant harm/damage.

The problem's outcomes might have become evident recently or some time ago, but have had harmful consequences if they have persisted for a long period of time.

Bringing the problem's ongoing consequences to your customer's attention is the key to trigger customers to make an immediate change between products to stop the damage as early as possible.

4. Wish creating questions:

Once your customer is aware of the problem's added consequences over time, then you need to create the wish for a means to stop the problem's added consequences. This would be done by asking pinpoint questions to create the customer's wish to have your solution, which is one that fills in the gaps.

You need to nurture the customer's interest in your product's extra features impacts, outcomes and related values which would fill in the gaps and stop the current damage.

5. Solution input using FIOV presentation model.

Now it's time to put the winning cards on your customer's table which already created in the previous step, and let your customer win the game and stop the damage.

To let your customer win the game, you should offer your solution using FIOV presentation model (explained in chapter 7) by highlighting the extra feature, impact, Outcome and related values compared against what the customer is presently using.

6. Break the customer: problem bond

As a last step you should encourage your customer to do a product trial, and to increase your product trial time frame to break the existing customer problem bond. A long trial period creates a new bond between the customer and your product.

4

Building rapport

Some industries are regulated, and the healthcare industry is a heavily-regulated environment. Close attention must be paid to the wording you use when you discuss pharmaceutical products with customers. Whether your industry is regulated or not, it is important to prepare your presentation in advance of your appointments, including how long your presentation will take. Showing up for appointments with customers without having properly prepared for the sales call with your guidelines in mind can lead to failure, whereas preparing and rehearsing will give you the confidence and flow of language which is essential for your sales call to be a success.

Building relationships with gatekeepers

One of the biggest challenges facing sales professionals is to get past the 'gatekeepers'. Those are the people who control access to your customer. They include your customer's office administrator, the manager of the practice and the receptionist. They are professionals and are well-trained to keep you away from meeting your sales lead or your target key opinion leader (KOL). They consider meetings with sales reps to be a waste of their co-worker's time and they would like to prove that they are the controllers. Their inclination is to deny any requests for appointments with your customer.

When you ask for an appointment, they usually ask what it would be regarding. Most sales reps would respond by saying that they have Important new information, or a new product and they would like to pass the information on.

The gatekeeper is likely to respond by saying that they are well-supplied or very happy with what they're using, and that new information can be sent by email or fax. Your chance to meet with your customer is over.

Getting past the gatekeepers is the crucial step in making a sales call. Here are some important tips for sales reps to get past the gatekeepers.

1. You must indicate that your relationship with them will last for a long time, since their facility is in your assigned sales region. So they would know that contacting them is not a one-time event.

    SELLER: "Hello. This is Mark Smith. I am your area representative from Company X. With whom am I speaking, please?"
    GATEKEEPER: "This is Sara."
    SELLER: "Thank you, Sara. I would like to have two minutes to meet with you and introduce myself and give you my business card. When would you be available?" (It's important to get their name, as a person's name is the door opener to building a relationship.)
    SARA: "Any time, I am here from 9 to 5 pm from Monday to Friday."

    Gatekeepers agree 100% about meeting with them because they realize that you are not going to do anything without their permission. This step starts earning their trust.

2. Build the relationship:
    When you meet with the gatekeeper, build rapport, grab their attention, and sound honest. Don't try to bypass the gatekeepers because you will lose credibility on the spot.

Thank them for their brief meeting. Give them your business card, and offer a compliment such as the person's pleasant voice over the phone. You want to sustain the momentum of the conversation.

3. Ask about their policy about meeting sales reps in the future when your company has a valuable solution for their patients or customers (for non-health-care related industries). Don't tell them that you already have a solution right now and you want to meet with the customer to talk about that solution.

   In this step you will discover what their policy is for scheduling meetings with customers and KOLs. For example, some practices prefer lunch-and-learn meetings while others prefer to meet at the end of the day or very early in the morning. It's important to acknowledge that you understand their policy and that you will abide by it.

4. Thank them and promise that you will be in touch to support them in helping their patients to get better outcomes. Leave the impression that you will only contact them when you have a product that will be of value to them/their patients or customers. This shows them that you are not pushy and that you value their time.

Let one or two weeks pass and then contact Sara again. A personal meeting is better than a telephone discussion. Ask that the KOL attend since you promised that you'd only visit if you had a great solution that would improve patient outcomes and increase their practice's credibility. Be sure to ask for the best date and time and how much time they would be setting aside for your visit. If you follow this procedure, you will get your appointment every time.

Not much chemistry here. You need to show the gatekeeper that you know they are the controllers and that you will respect their rules. At the same time, you as a sales professional are showing your value as a good source of information that will enhance their practice.

Gaining a gatekeeper's trust is far better than getting past him or her. If you didn't earn their trust but somehow got past them once, you will never be successful in the future attempts.

One of the most important first steps for your call success is to adapt to the situation and build rapport with your customer. Building rapport is a must for your call success whether interacting with gate-keepers or with customers/KOLs (key opinion leaders). People like to be listened to. They like to talk about themselves, their experiences, their lives, families, weather; what they like and what they don't like; they like to talk about what they care about and like to share their points of views. People tend to be more conservative in any new business relationship so the most important step you need to do is to build the customer's confidence in you. Once confidence has been established then the door will be opened to build a long-term relationship. There is a difference between trust and confidence, and most often confidence is what develops after a number of events or inquiries that required trust turned out as expected. A good history of trustworthiness from a sales rep leads customers to develop confidence in that rep. Understand that confidence is a willingness to commit to something that you are already certain about. That's what confidence is. Trust is a willingness to commit yourself to the unknown, which is why confidence is such a significant and meaningful word.

It's very important to reach beyond your customer's trust level to his or her confidence level so that he or she starts to rely on you. Confidence results from repeated trusted events with the sales professional. Rapport is not about the value you bring. It's about having something in common that makes you easily get along with the other person. It makes your customer feel that he/she would love to see you again and again. To build excellent rapport, you need to discover your customers' interests - what they like, and what they like to talk about. Some customers like to talk about politics, some like to talk about their social life, hockey games, golfing, TV shows, films.

Mutual interests

In one interesting situation, I decided to research the customer I was going to meet with. She was a family physician and I hoped to secure her business. I looked up her profile on Facebook and discovered that she was a fan of the television show *House*. I researched the show and found it interesting. I downloaded a picture of Dr. Gregory house (Hugh Laurie) and the show's cast to my cell phone's home page. I made an appointment with her, and once there, I positioned my cell phone so that she could see the image. Before even starting our discussion, she said, "Do you like this show?" I said, "Yes, I love it. Do you?" She talked about the show for almost 20 minutes. I shared some funny comments about the show which she enjoyed, and then she asked me to come by the next morning at 11:00 am to discuss our new product. My scheduled time with her was set for half hour but because of the common interest in the TV show, she was willing to spend more time with me, adding 15 minutes. This physician was classified in our company as 'class B' based on her prescription behaviour and loyalty towards our company. She started prescribing my medication an average of 5 to 10 packs per day. As we became friends and the bond became stronger, her prescriptions reached up to 500 packs per month. She was re-classified as a 'class A' customer.

Always pay attention to the pictures or certificates that your customers have on their office walls or desks. They will give you an idea about what credentials they have, what they are interested in and what they care about.

People love to get compliments, receive praise and admiration for their credentials, or what they wear, or their hair style.

It doesn't hurt if your customer plays golf. You could play a round of golf together, but pay attention to the game, and don't ever talk about business. Make it a fun atmosphere.

Sympathy

Sympathy is a great word in building a great relationship. It's the sense of compassion, and it's when you feel badly for someone who is going through pain or a hard situation. Sympathy is what differentiates us as humans. It's simply a feeling of support.

I was working as a sales and marketing director for a multinational company, and I decided to make an appointment with an important prospect. Based on my research I knew that she recently left her position in one company and moved to a new company. She was working as a quality control manager for a multinational company.

I introduced myself over the phone, and started with this sentence: *"Congratulations on the new position. You made the right choice for this move."* I thought that the call would take five minutes- just long enough to set up the appointment - but to my surprise the call took over 45 minutes because of my opening sentence. She acknowledged that she had made the right choice and started mentioning why she left her position in detail and the pain she went through with the previous employer.

I agreed with what she said and felt sympathetic, as I would have done the same thing if I had been in her position. I felt that she had done the right thing and I told her so. In one week, I got a business contract from her starting with $400,000 for just the first three months alone, (and her business is still on-going).

Components of building confidence and rapport

Share customer beliefs

Ascertain what your customer's beliefs are and see if you can relate a story from your own life that reflects your customer's beliefs. Share your commitment to keeping promises and fulfilling their product needs and wishes with a goal toward improving work flow and getting greater results for them and their patients.

1. Mention a real success story about how you provided outstanding customer support and how it made a big difference for your customer.
2. Make sure the customer knows that you value him or her and that what your customer is paying for is not your service but the quality of your service.
3. Be specific in your questions by asking pinpoint questions so your customer will understand that you are expert in their field, so they can rely on you.

Active listening

1. Show interest by actively listening to your customer.
2. Use sympathy. Emphasize and paraphrase what your customer has said because it shows them that you understand their point of view.
3. Understand your customer's practice and the issues they might have. Act as a resource partner for your customer and offer the best solution.
4. Make a support intervention using body language such as nodding and verbalizing.

Continuous communication

1. Sales reps need to be versatile. They must be able to adapt to any situation.
2. Your integrity is crucial. Always be honest and have strong moral principles.
3. Focus on customer priorities. It will help in building great rapport.
4. Your knowledge plays a role in building rapport. Keep yourself up-to-date about market trends, your products and competitors' products. People tend to listen closely for new and valuable information.

People tend to give business to salespeople who they can trust and who can fulfill their promises and keep their word. People tend to be confident about sales people who are attentive to their needs and satisfy them.

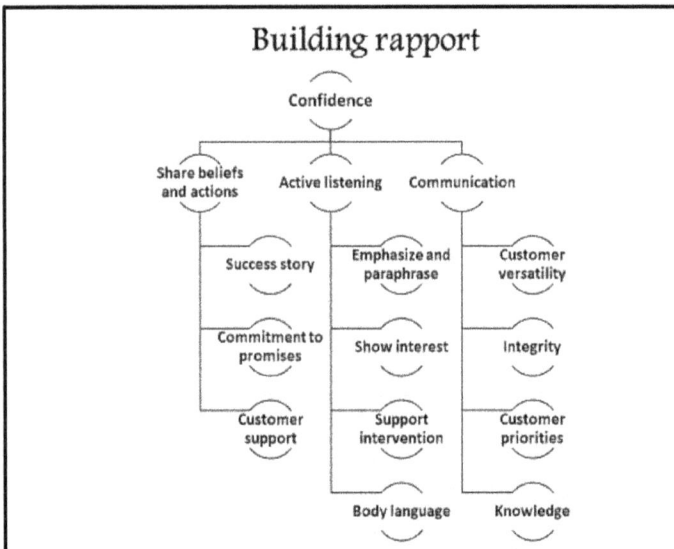

Building rapport

Attention grabbers

An attention grabber is one of the most important steps to secure your customer's attention. It is an opening statement containing multiple sentences intended to grab a customer's attention and get the customer

engaged in the conversation. In this step, we don't mention anything about our products or their features, or impacts.

An attention grabber consists of four interconnected sentences. It begins with a general introduction that is related to a common problem that is related to a supposed general need or wish that a typical customer (or patient) has, and it concludes with a position statement.

Here's an example of an attention grabber.

You are introducing a hormonal replacement medication to a gynecology specialist. It is your first call to the specialist.

> SELLER: "Hi Dr. Smith, I'm here today to present a great solution *(Value statement)* which has helped 200,000 patients suffering from menopause symptoms to get relief and enjoy their daily life activities. I would like to share great solution's outcome with you and get your feedback as well."
>
> DR. SMITH: "Go ahead."
>
> SELLER: *(This is the general introduction.)* In most doctor's practices, the physicians see many women suffering from hot flashes, intercourse pain, and night sweats, which is all very annoying especially given the average age of onset of menopause is 50 years old. (Pause). They always wish for a better solution to help those patients.

(This is the *supposed general need statement*.) "Improving a patient's lifestyle is the main goal for getting them back to their daily activities."

(This is the position statement.) "Then they can regain happiness and self-confidence." (Pause to allow your customer to become engaged in the conversation.)

The attention grabber has two main parts: the opening statement and its sub-parts; the attention-grabber and its four sub-sentences.

1. Opening Statement:
a) Value statement:
> Value statement must include the value you could offer to your customer (e.g., offer a great solution which has helped 200,000 patients overcome menopause symptoms).

Value statements grab a customer's interest in discovering how the solution impacted those patients and the customer will want to ask questions and to be asked as well.

b) The agenda for the call:

The sales rep. needs to point out the main topics to be discussed. This helps your customer stay focused and ready to engage in a discussion (e.g., about a great solution's outcome in controlling common menopause symptoms and, to elicit the doctor's experience dealing with those patients and getting his/her feedback about the new solution you are offering).

c) Customer's approval to proceed with the sales call:

Getting the customer's approval to proceed with the presentation ensures that your customer is comfortable listening and engaging in a two-way conversation. This could be done by mentioning the previous call's agenda in a form of question.

2. Attention grabber body:

The attention grabber's body includes four sentences.

a) General introduction:

The goal of the general introduction along with a general related problem in the attention grabber body is to increase awareness about the existence of the problem. (Please review the value underlying the Awareness step and its explanation in chapter 3.) Then, express what your company offers to solve this problem for this customer just as it successfully solved the same problem in other practices. This will create a comfort level for physicians, an expectation that they will be able to resolve this problem for their patients. In the previous example, the general introduction sentence is "Most doctors see many patients suffering from menopause symptoms."

b) General related problem:

The general problem in the previous example would be the menopause symptoms which are very annoying. (increase awareness about a common existing problem)

c) Supposed general wish or need:

This would be improved sense of comfort and wellness and a return to their normal daily activities, in the current example. The need for either the patient or the doctor is to get the patient healthier so that she is better able to engage in daily life activities.

d) Position statement:

In this statement you set your solution apart from the others. It could be described as your product personality - how you would describe your product and what makes it unique. It could be one or two words which stick in everyone's mind when you mention your drug's name, such as 'regain patient's happiness and self-confidence'. These two words help build your brand name by bringing happiness and self-confidence to women suffering from menopause symptoms.

Attention grabbers are a part of the APWS Selling Method. However, there is another pitch that would work perfectly; it's short, simple and grabs attention:

Example 1:

"Dr. James, I am here to share a great patient outcomes' solution to eliminate menopause symptoms, and reduce the risk of associated drug side effects and help get your patients back to their daily happy life activities."

The rule here is to focus on a valued extra feature's impact, outcome and related value for both the patient and the physician compared with what they are currently using or prescribing.

Do you see a difference between example 1 and example 2 below?

Example 2:

Sales Rep.: "Dr. James, I am here today to tell you about a new solution for handling menopause symptoms."

Did the sales rep. in example 2 offer an extra feature's impact and outcome compared to what the physician is presently using? No, the listener might lose interest in the rest of the call. Also, the sales rep. mentioned the word 'new' which can raise red flags for the customer.

In example 1, the sales rep mentioned the meeting agenda with two features and the corresponding impacts which grab customer attention.

Your meeting agenda
Share a solutions' outcomes
And reduce risk of associated drugs

Product's features and impact

Feature 1: Eliminate menopause symptoms

Impact: Regain self-confidence.

Feature 2: Reduce risk of associated drug side effects

Impact: Happiness and enjoyment of daily life activities
Remember to pause two or three seconds to let your customer think and engage. The most successful call involves two-way communication or what we call a 'conversational' style between you and your customer.

5

Uncovering the Need or the Wish

After the introduction of the attention grabber, you should uncover the interests and concerns of your customer by asking pinpoint questions. Questions should be focused on engaging your customer towards your product's solution. If you are offering a new product which has no competitors, then you need to create the customer's interest in a solution to an existing problem. If you offer a product which has competitors, then you need to create a customer's interest in an extra feature's impact and related outcome compared to the competitor's product. This is what I refer to as *wish creation*.

PROBING WITH OPEN-ENDED QUESTIONS

Correct approach leads to a revealed need	Wrong approach
Rep's Questions	**Rep's Questions**
• How do you usually deal with this patient's needs?	• Do you consider hormonal therapy in your regimen? (the answer could be NO and your chance of winning is getting lower)
• Which patients do you prefer to consider for prescribing hormonal replacement therapy?	• How often do you see patients suffering from hot flashes? (remember, he is a gynaecologist and sees such patients daily; don't waste the time in asking for an obvious answer).
• What are the most important criteria you consider for prescribing such medication?	• What kind of medication are you prescribing? (that's considered an interfering question with your customer's protocol especially if asked in a group presentation).

Tips about these questions

Don't ask questions that can be answered using *yes* or *no*. Your questions should begin with *what*, or *how*. A question that begins with *why* is not advisable because it can make your customers feel as though they are being interrogated. You are not an investigator. You need to encourage your customers to share their experiences with you so that you understand their perspectives and priorities. The only time you should use a question that would yield a *yes* response will be when you are dealing with an indifferent personality. Limit the number of questions to two or three especially in the pharmaceutical industry. By contrast, you can expect to ask far more questions in a complex sale, such as when selling medical devices, so as to better understand your customer's problems and issues. Otherwise, the customer may get annoyed and feel that your call is taking too long, and you may soon find that you are being interrupted and rushed. Pause after each question, as previously mentioned, to let your customer think and engage in the discussion. Develop your listening skills and focus on what your customer is saying. Listen effectively to the interests or concerns in order to discover the customer's needs. Don't ask complex questions. Always ask one question at a time to avoid any confusion. Don't ever interrupt while your customer is answering your questions, as it shows disrespect.

Refrain from asking questions that might make your customer feel his or her knowledge or professionalism is being challenged. For example: "What's your protocol in treating those patients or what are the medications you are prescribing for your patients?" might get you a shocking answer like "It's none of your business" or you might just be met with total silence. You might be perceived as interfering in something personal especially if you asked that question in a group meeting. Your customer might not answer or might remain silent for a few seconds as each physician has his or her own protocol which they may not wish to reveal. If so, simply change the question.

Support intervention

As explained before, once you have the revealed need or wish related to your product's features and impact, you must do something called *support intervention*.

Communicating your understanding involves letting the other person know that you are listening effectively and that you understand his/her point of view. This will increase your credibility and enhance mutual respect. It also helps you to build trust and a long-term relationship.

Support intervention creates a level of comfort and an atmosphere of co-operation. It's a result of active listening to what has been said. Active listening is the first step in doing support intervention, which involves the listener observing the speaker's behavior and body language. Having the ability to interpret a person's body language lets the listener develop a more accurate understanding of the speaker's message. Having heard, the listener may then paraphrase the speaker's words.

Example of support intervention:

> CUSTOMER: "The most important thing to me is to have an effective product with minimal side effects."
>
> SELLER: "I absolutely agree with you." *(a support intervention)* "Healing as fast as possible *(Impact on efficacy)*

along with safety *(Impact of minimal side effects)* are very crucial for much better outcomes" (paraphrased).

This statement will put you in the customer's shoes, and it helps customers get in touch with their feelings or attitudes. It creates rapport, opens the lines of communication and encourages discussion and further sharing. It also predisposes your customer to accept what you are going to say.

Things to avoid during probing:

Your call is time-sensitive

- Asking many probing questions can be annoying and give the impression of prolonging the call. You might be interrupted and get rushed by your customer and lose your concentration and the call as well.

Your attitude

- Avoid negative, apologetic and/or a teaching attitude, or you might face rejection and more objections. Always use consultative approach.

Listening Skills

- Talking without pausing will prevent your customer from engaging. You want customers to engage.

Avoid one way conversation

- Your call must be conversational, not one-sided only from you. People like to talk more than listen to you.

Asking very specific questions

- Example: "What are you prescribing for your patients?" You might face silence for more than the usual time. If you made it by mistake, simply change the question.

Avoid multiple or compound questions

- Leads to confusion and distraction.

Avoid leading questions

- Could be answered by "No" , Only use these with indifferent personalities (described later)

Never criticize your competitors

Exercise 1. Selling Simulation

Your Client

You have an appointment with Dr. Expert, a busy family physician with an older practice in your city. She sees a lot of patients with diabetes who are also overweight/obese. While Dr. Expert recognizes that obesity is recognized as a cardiovascular risk to patients with diabetes, she hasn't been very successful in helping her diabetic patients lose weight. Dr. Expert is skeptical about new solutions and needs to be convinced about safety and efficacy.

Your Product
You are a pharmaceutical sales representative introducing a new product called Magic that will help patients lose weight and better control their diabetes. You have some creative leeway here to "invent" a product profile, so have fun!

Your Brochure
Put together a one-page brochure you would use to support your message to sell to Dr. Expert.

Your Task
Prepare a selling discussion for Magic which incorporates your brochure and be prepared to sell Dr. Expert some Magic.

Presentation:

Once you've done the support intervention, it's time to present your product.

Presentation of the product should be based on the customer-revealed need or wish that you already have already discovered.

Focus always on the feature, impacts, outcomes and values of your product.

Once you have an answer to your open-ended questions, you must communicate and understand. Let the other person know that you understand his or her point of view by doing the following three steps:

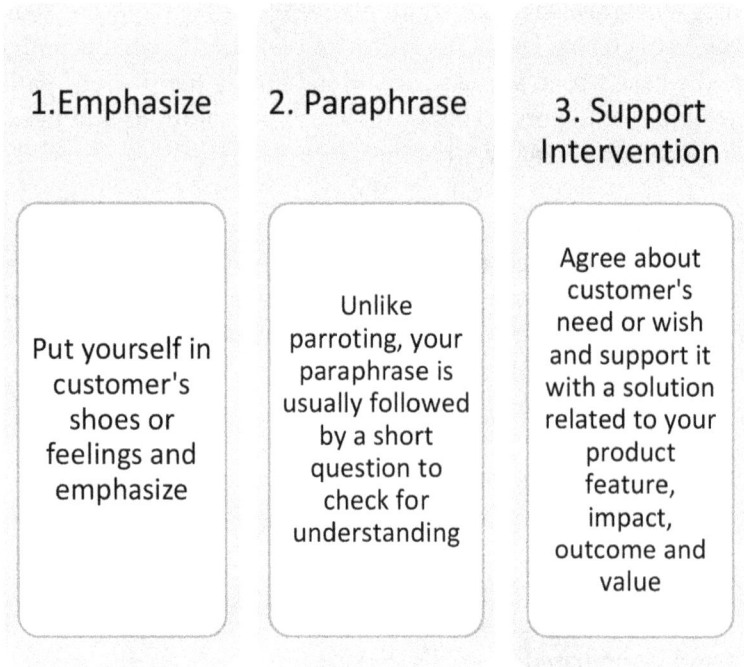

1.Emphasize	2. Paraphrase	3. Support Intervention
Put yourself in customer's shoes or feelings and emphasize	Unlike parroting, your paraphrase is usually followed by a short question to check for understanding	Agree about customer's need or wish and support it with a solution related to your product feature, impact, outcome and value

An example:

Magic is your first line of choice for obesity control and treatment. The only once-daily combination clinically proven to significantly reduce weight.

LIVE SAFER AND REGAIN CONFI-DENCE

Magic was studied in two large FDA-approved trials that involved 2,700 patients whose BMI (body mass index) was 30 kg/m² with two or more weight-related co- morbidities such as hypertension, type 2 diabetes mellitus, or dyslipidemia. Presented here are weight loss and waist circumference reductions of patients having a baseline BMI of 30 kg/m² or greater, and who used the study drug for the planned 56-week course of treatment. Patients were randomized to placebo and Magic (ingredient 1 and ingredient 2).

Magic efficacy

BMI>30KG/M2 AFTER 1 YEAR

Placebo · Starting dose 2.5 mg

Recommended dose 5mg · Top dose 10 mg

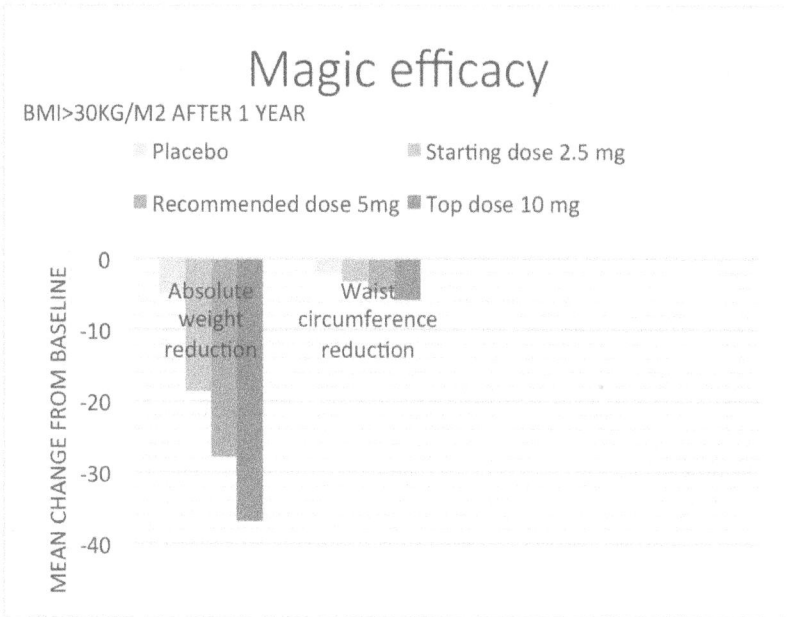

Magic was the first weight-loss prescription approved in the past 13 years.

2.2 million prescriptions for Magic have been filled to help patients achieve their weight-loss goals.

The only one combination pill clinically proven by the FDA for chronic weight management.

Magic has the highest safety profile compared to the weight loss gold standard products.

Incidence of 4 side effects in 370 patients after 56 weeks of treatment

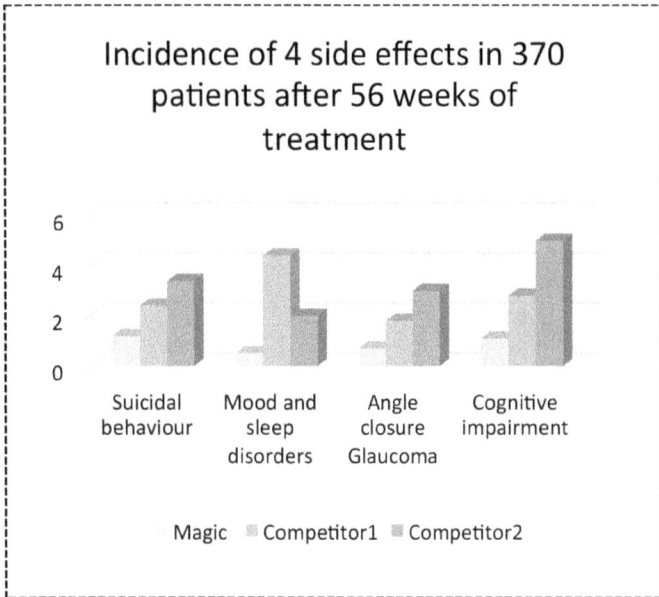

XYZ Journal, August 2018

Magic has made significant improvement for 650 diabetic patients having the following profiles: blood pressure, cholesterol and triglycerides.

blood pressure
- From average 160/95
- To average 130/ 83

cholesterol
- From average 6.7 mmol/L
- To average 3.5 mmol/L

triglycerides
- From average 5.8 mmol/L
- To average 1.6 mmol/L

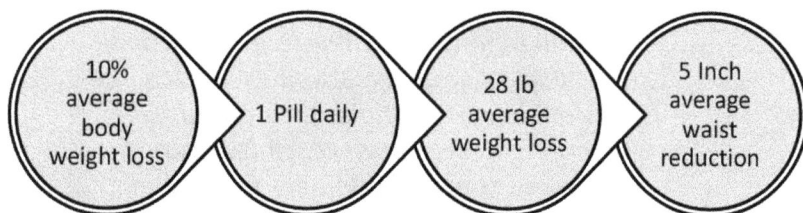

Explanation:

Imagine that this is your product's visual aid, and your doctor's *wish* was about safety and efficacy. You must focus on absolute weight reduction, waist circumference reduction and side effects compared to the competitors. No need to mention the rest except the dose. Remember that you might have two or three minutes to complete your presentation, or sometimes as little as 30 seconds or as long as 15 minutes. It could be longer depending upon your customer's level of engagement in the discussion. This is a good time to ask a question like, *How does that sound?* And then pause to hear their responses. Or you could ask, *How do these outcomes compare with what you have been using?* And then pause. Always let your customer get engaged by asking a question and waiting for a response. If the *need* was to pay attention to Magic's safety profile in diabetic patients, you should focus on the effect on diabetic patients and the impact on the blood pressure, cholesterol, triglycerides and side effects compared to the results of competitors' products.

Let's start with greeting Dr. Expert and then build rapport by asking a few questions.

Remember the rule:

Think about making a general introduction related to a general problem that is related to a general supposed wish or a need, supported by a position statement.

> *"(general introduction) Dr. Expert, in*
> *your practice you see many diabetic patients*
> *suffering from obesity (pause). (general*
> *problem) The rapidly-rising prevalence of*

obesity is alarming. It predisposes patients to co-morbidities like hypertension, serious cardiovascular diseases, and dyslipidemias. Lifestyle modifications alone might have very limited success, which (supposed need or wish) *necessitates the addition of pharmacotherapy to help obese diabetic patients live safer, healthier lives and to* (position statement) *regain confidence and enjoy their daily life activities."*

Another opening:

"(Value statement) *Dr. Expert, I am here today to offer a great solution which has helped 100,000* (General related problem) *diabetic obese patients so far to* (Supposed need or wish) *reduce their weight, reduce their risk of cardiovascular diseases in obese diabetic patients as well as reduce the risk of weight loss products to help your patients* (Position statement) *live safer and healthier lives."*

So, I would be grateful to you if you would share with me some of your experience in handling weight loss in diabetic patients.

Dr. Expert: "Yes sure."

SALES REP: QUESTION #1: "What criteria would you use to choose between two medications for weight loss?" (Need creation)

QUESTION #2: How do you judge the efficacy between two products for a weight loss? (Need creation)

QUESTION #3: How do you measure the safety between two products for weight loss with your diabetic patients? (Need creation)

Important tips about probing questions

Questions must lead to a supposed *wish* or *need* which matches your product's impacts and outcomes. The customer is looking for solutions to his or her patient's problems.

> FOR QUESTION #1, the presumed answer would be safety and efficacy, then you have a golden opportunity to match these two needs to your product's efficacy and safety.
>
> FOR QUESTION #2, the presumed answer would be the time frame for weight loss, then you support it with the clinical trial and efficacy compared to placebo in a specific time period.
>
> FOR QUESTION #3, the presumed answer would be fewer side effects, at which point you have a great chance to speak about fewer side effects from your product when compared to the gold standard.

The previous examples were examples of an introduction, attention grabber and need creation questions.

And likely you will get an answer such as:

> *Dr. Expert: "Well, safety and efficacy are very important to me, especially weight loss products in diabetic patients. They could have serious side effects on health and could kill if they have a low safety profile, so we need to keep the patient on a low regimen and monitor the patient on a regular basis. I tend to use chemical formula products on a short-term basis, unless they're well trialed, and use diet and natural products on most patients."*

How are you going to reply to Dr. Expert's response?

You must identify the areas of concerns or fear which need to be addressed and areas of interests which need to be supported and validated. Areas of interest are considered *wishes* if your customer is using a direct competitor, and they're considered *needs* if the customer is presently using a different product that has a totally different mechanism of action.

Dr. Expert's areas of interest are:

- A proof of high safety profile
- A proof of high efficacy
- Low regimen
- Supportive trials on safety

Dr. Expert's areas of concerns:

- The use of chemical formulations that have low safety profiles on diabetic patients.
- High dosages.
- Using a product with not enough clinical trials.

So, what will your next step be?

- Provide support intervention.
- Paraphrase.
- Present the related features, impacts, outcomes and values (FIOV) to address Dr. Expert's interests and focus on eliminating the concerns.

Remember the KISS rule (keep it short and simple and to the points of interest)

You can reply as follows:

> SALES REP: *"(Support intervention)* You are absolutely right. A high safety profile with those patients along with efficacy are the top priorities. Especially with Magic which given on a low regimen once daily was enough to get the desired effect, as you can see."

Present:

> SALES REP: *(FIOV Technique)* "*(Feature)* Magic has the highest safety profile compared to the gold standard drugs

in the market in terms of *(Feature's Outcomes)* suicidal behavior, cognitive impairment, mood and sleep disorders and secondary glaucoma. These findings were published in XYZ magazine in (month) 2015. (Show on brochure), and that leads to *(Value)* much better patient outcomes. *(APOC technique)* Would that work much better for your patients?"

DR. EXPERT: "It depends on the clinical studies."

(This is a buying signal)

SALES REP: "Definitely, yes, clinical studies are supporting the claim *(support intervention)*. Magic's efficacy was clinically proven in an FDA study on 2700 patients for 56 weeks, the study shows that Magic at the recommended dose has a significant absolute weight reduction and waist circumference reduction compared to placebo, *(show brochure)*, which leads to life style improvement and less cardiovascular risk. *(Engage)* How does that sound?"

DR. EXPERT: "Sounds good so far. Are there any precautions that have been taken during the treatment for diabetic patients?" *(A buying signal)*

SALES REP: *(Cite a professional organization)* "The FDA study shows that no special precautions have been taken at the recommended dose, as it has a very high safety profile, and studies show that Magic has a significant improvement on blood pressure, cholesterol and triglycerides in a trial on 650 diabetic patients. (Show results in brochure).

SALES REP: "Have I answered your question to your satisfaction?"

DR. EXPERT: "Absolutely."

The Close and The commitment

SALES REP: *(asking commitment-leading question)*: "We have discussed Magic. Would you please give me an example of the type of patient who best suits Magic?"

DR. EXPERT: "Yes, I think it best suits patients coming for follow-up for whom the existing regimen doesn't work well."

Prioritize Features and Impacts in your Presentation

If we look at the presentation, we placed priority on mentioning safety because Dr. Expert's focus was on safety, and then on efficacy, as he mentioned it alongside safety.

In the middle of the presentation he asked about the precautions (remember he is skeptical about the safety and efficacy), so it was important to reiterate the high safety profile and the effect on the blood work as proof of diabetic patient improvement.

One-minute sales call:

Sometimes customers tell you that you have 30 seconds or 60 seconds to present your product to them. The best way to use such limited time is to focus on mentioning indications, any precautions, the dose and the cost.

Here's an example that uses hormonal therapy. Applying this advice for an exceedingly brief presentation:

> **SALES REP:** *"Product X is used for the control of vasomotor symptoms in a dose of 2 mg once a day, no common side effects to worry about, and it costs only 15 cents per tablet."*

Finally, you must hand him over the FDA study as a proof on the safety and efficacy or any other material that supports your claims.

The previous exercise is an example of a typical sales call with a passive behavior personality, but you need to know what kind of personalities you could meet during a sales presentation. Remember, selling is not a neat process: objections, questions and concerns can be raised at any time during the sales call so be prepared.

6

Customer Personality and Behaviour Types

People sometimes confuse behavior with personality. We are born with a personality. It is shaped by genetics and environment. Behavior, by contrast, is learnt, and our behavior changes throughout life based on experiences, interactions and our mood at any given time. There is no such thing as only being one type, as we in fact use all types of behavior. The more interactive your life with others, the greater the chance you use all types of behavior in a day.

The Skeptic

Skeptics are people who do not believe or are not convinced of something until they have investigated the situation. They like and prefer to see reasons, clarifications, facts and proofs, and they never get convinced based on assumptions. They like to see evidence that supports theories. Once all facts are in, they become firm believers. They might ask you a lot of questions and it might seem like an interrogation, but don't get annoyed because that's just how skeptics are.

Skeptics are not necessarily lacking in imagination, but they prefer to live in the real world, and they depend on factual thinking.

If you want to grab a skeptic's attention, just give him a piece of the information and supportive evidence. If (s)he is interested, expect that (s)he will require additional time to investigate and confirm the information before making any decision. If you meet skeptics in a sales call, they will want supportive written evidence, such as a published study from a reputable organization or reports published in public media such as newspapers.

The advantage of this personality type is that skeptics are easy to deal with, they are usually honest, straightforward and have a strong work ethic.

How to deal with skeptics:

1. don't argue
2. provide proof, like a published article in a journal or magazine, to back up your claims

The Acceptor

This personality is classified as agreeable. Acceptors tend to be sympathetic, co-operative, and warm. They tend to perceive others in a positive light, are more emotionally responsive, and like to help other people. They are usually the extroverts of this world and they gain energy in social situations. They listen and accept the circumstances and usually don't ask many questions, which is in sharp contrast to passive personalities who could interrogate you more or might not even be listening (to be further explained in the section about passive personalities). Acceptors are very easy personalities to deal with. Sum up the features and impacts, outcomes and values and take the commitment (make the sale).

The Objector

This personality tends to be careful and deliberate. Objectors tend to discuss issues carefully. They object because they are seeking more information. They plan well and they need to be efficient in everything they do, which is why they object – so as to get more details.

Dealing with this personality will be explained in detail in the section about resolving objections.

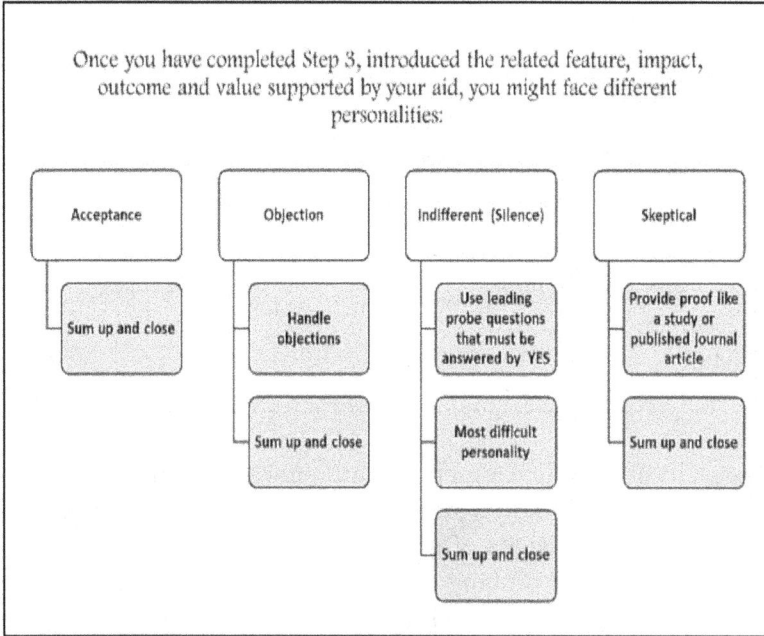

Once you have completed Step 3, introduced the related feature, impact, outcome and value supported by your aid, you might face different personalities:

Acceptance	Objection	Indifferent (Silence)	Skeptical
Sum up and close	Handle objections	Use leading probe questions that must be answered by YES	Provide proof like a study or published journal article
	Sum up and close	Most difficult personality	Sum up and close
		Sum up and close	

The Indifferent Personality

This is the most difficult personality to deal with. Our research shows that 75% of sales calls involving indifferent personalities end in failure because the sales reps don't know how to handle this kind of personality. Your customer could be indifferent by nature or may choose to be indifferent during your sales call. Indifferent or apathetic customers tend to be quiet and reserved. Such customers create a communication barrier by not paying attention to what they are being told. They generally prefer interacting with a few close friends rather than a wide circle of acquaintances, and they expend energy in social situations (whereas extroverts gain energy).

Agreeable positive outcomes technique
(APOC)

How should you deal with indifferent personalities in a sales call?

Indifferent or apathetic people tend to be quiet and reserved.

This is the most difficult personality to deal with and most sales professionals get tripped up by these personalities.

The customer remains silent so as to avoid interacting with you and avoids showing any signs of interest.

Your indifferent customers usually remain silent during your presentations and avoid engaging in the presentation. The customer avoids showing any signs of interest, and may sometimes rush you when you start your probing questions so as to end your call. Such customers may give excuses, citing an important meeting or appointment that is going to start soon. They may just claim to be very busy. They may be offering these reasons to conclude your sales call for any of the following reasons:

- They are firmly entrenched in using a competing product.
- They are satisfied with what they are presently using.
- They have a good relationship with your competitor's rep or management.
- They had a bad experience with your company, sales rep or management, and in this case, they might be hostile to your product too.
- They might have been given misleading/incorrect information about your product from your competitor.

What is the best way to deal with indifferent personalities? Some trainers say that the best action here is to focus on the features and

benefits of your products, but again, such customers will still be quiet and unengaged so how are you going to engage them and secure their commitment to your products? Try the APOC technique.

Agreeable Positive Outcomes Commitment technique (APOC)

Sales professionals used to apply a technique in sales called tie-down, the remedy is to ask your customer little questions along the way and monitor the feedback. Doesn't that make sense? You know what I mean? Are you following me? Wouldn't you agree? Is that right? This simple technique serves to tie a statement down."

It was a great technique in the 1970s, however, using this technique doesn't necessarily work in your favor. Most of the time the customer realizes that the sales rep is trying to lead her/him to say yes. Customers are very intelligent and can pick this up, and customers will say yes simply to avoid embarrassing the sales rep, but in doing so, it leads to the customer providing a false agreement.

In our competitive selling environment and given new, aggressive competitors nowadays, it was necessary to implement a new technique which would enable the sales professional not only to get the customer's feedback but to engage indifferent personalities and lead to a smooth close. In addition, sales professionals were in need of a technique to be used for quick closes when limited call time was available.

In this new technique, make sure that you ask a question that includes a feature, a feature's impact, outcome and a related value. Doing so will ensure that the customer will agree on the value he would benefit from, not just because you need to hear the word yes.

So, the best approach to dealing with indifferent personalities is to apply the Agreeable Positive Outcomes Commitment technique. In this technique, you encourage your customer to be engaged, you mention a positive outcome and corresponding value that the customer must agree with and can't object to. You start with a leading probe question. A leading probe question is a question that leads the customer to a specific answer - an answer that you want, and which favors your product(s).

After presenting your introduction and attention grabber, and asking probing questions, your indifferent personality type customer remains quiet, as expected.

SELLER: "Do you think your patients would appreciate a product which doesn't cause abdominal pain, so they would be more comfortable using it?"

INDIFFERENT: The only reasonable answer is yes, absolutely

SELLER: "Do you think that giving one capsule per day is more convenient for your diabetic patients?"

INDIFFERENT: The only reasonable answer is yes, absolutely.

SELLER: "What do you think about prescribing a medication which minimizes cognitive impairment and suicidal behavior? Would it be safer compared to the gold standards?"

INDIFFERENT: The only reasonable answer is yes, definitely.

The point here is to let your customer agree about positive outcomes - outcomes that any reasonable person would have to agree with, which then nearly forces the customer to commit to using or prescribing your product.

Note: Make sure that you state the feature and its outcome and related value in each question.

Using this approach, you are guiding your customer toward a positive commitment and you will have the green light for a smooth close.

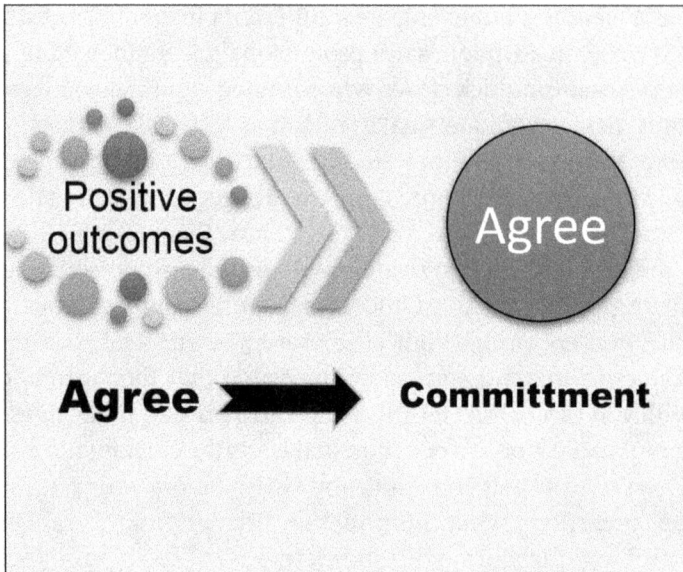

Indifferent personality technique

You could use APOC too with any personality when the sales situation seems to be difficult to close. In addition, use it when you have a limited time for the sales call.

Practice the APOC technique. Be sure to prepare your questions in advance. Try it and have fun. You will be amazed!!

Different behaviors you encounter during your sales calls

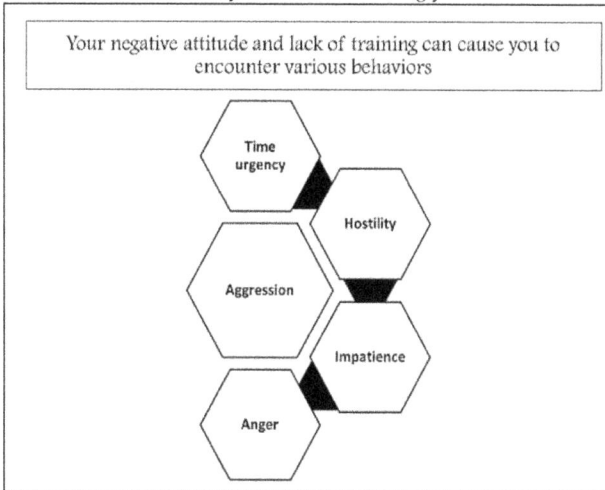

Different customer behaviors:

To be successful in your sales call, you must understand human behavior. Remember that a customer may exhibit different behavior when (s)he meets you alone compared to when there are other people present at a meeting. You might be surprised to see that a customer looks calm and quiet in a one-on-one setting yet behaves aggressively when in a group meeting (see below: passive-aggressives or 'alternators').

The Passive behavior:

Positive-passive acceptor:

The customer who has a passive behavior may be one of the easiest customer behaviors to deal with if the person is passive but actively listens to you. A good sign that your customer is actively listening is evident when (s)he gets engaged in the discussion and asks you questions to clarify or better understand something.

Negative-passive acceptor:

On the other hand, this behavior could be difficult to handle if the person fails to actively listen, in which case the person tries to avoid any conflict by agreeing with what has been said yet (s)he didn't really focus on what you were saying and considered your words as being background noise. As another indicator, they might avoid making eye contact.

The key to dealing with a passive person who is not actively listening is to ask her/him questions during your presentations to make sure that they understand and to get them to engage in the presentation. I also recommend using the APOC technique near the end of the presentation for an effective close.

The Aggressive behavior:

The aggressive style is all about control and dominance. Aggressive customers feel that they must control a situation, be right, and 'win'. To satisfy these needs, they use aggression to feel powerful and in control by trying to take control of everyone around them.

Situations that create aggression include:

1. If the customer feels that the information you are providing is meant to make up for the customer's (judged-to-be) inadequate knowledge.
2. Any attempts to condemn what (s)he is currently prescribing.
3. Any objections you express contrary to what the customer claims or asserts.
4. Any past negative experiences with a sales representative or bad customer service experience from a company.

What should you do? Here are some good strategies:

- Use support intervention: paraphrasing and emphasize; listen carefully to what the customer is saying and use sentences that begin with "Yes, and..." while avoiding sentences that begin with or include "Yes, but...".
- Ask the customer about his or her experiences with your company. Use the customer's name. A person's name is the doorway into their world; a person's name has the power to open

a connection into their world; it is a connection to show them who you are, and a connection to show them how you see them. A person's name has power over them, more than you might think.

- Avoid preaching and never condemn your competitor.

Alternating or Passive-Aggressive Behavior

Alternating behavior is simply the combination of both of the above: being passive and aggressive. Alternating behavior can often be found in people with mood and personality disorders. They struggle to regulate their behavior to one type primarily, and instead are either passive or aggressive. This behavior isn't common, but you will sometimes encounter those who display it.

The passive-aggressive style is all about harboring and bottling one's emotions. The person is usually full of anger, yet will mask it with a smile, not finding time to do a favor he promised, such as prescribing your drug, routinely refusing appointments, or perhaps doing something poorly to get out of an appointment in the future. These are all examples of passive-aggressive behaviors. The customer fails to own what (s)he did by claiming to have forgotten. The key to dealing with such personalities is to be positive and calm. Passive-aggressive people can twist your words using technicalities if you speak too generally, so always be specific when you ask for commitment or an action. For example, if the customer agrees to try your product, you need to respond by asking 'how many patients, and for how long?'

Start the conversation about the issue, and if your customer promised to do something but in fact did the reverse, make sure to ask why.

Be an assertive communicator by showing respect and confidence.

Make sure to acknowledge the value of the customer's experience so that the sales call will not end in failure.

Things to consider during your sales call to avoid undesirable behaviours

Sympathy

"...nature has given to man one tongue, but two ears, that we may hear from others as much as we speak." Epictetus

Flow of language

Be well-prepared

Positive attitude

Always be positive

Listening skills

Don't interrupt

Interpersonal skills

Here are some examples of ways to pose a question with the reaction you could get from each.

QUESTION 1: May I ask you a couple of questions.

QUESTION 2: Would you please share with me some of your experiences dealing with those patients?

Which one sounds better? The second one which encourages him to speak with confidence and values his/her experience:

QUESTION 1: Would you promise to try our drug on the next five patients?

QUESTION 2: From what has been discussed, which patients are the ideal patients to use this drug?

Which sentence is most likely to lead our customer to making a commitment?

Again, it is the second sentence which should be used. It acknowledges the importance of the customer's opinion and experience.

ANSWER 1: Our product doesn't have this side effect at all.

ANSWER 2: I would like to follow up with you on this matter in the next visit. There has been no mention about this side effect from any of the other doctors, and the drug leaflet doesn't mention this specific side effect. Please let me know how many of your other patients show the same side effect. How does that sound?

Which sentence sounds better?

The second response to claims of side effects is a more professional answer and shows that you acknowledge and respect the physician's claims and ask for the physician's commitment to continue prescribing the drug and report any more side effects to you. Responding in this manner greatly reduces the chances that the physician will reject the product completely and develop an aggressive attitude that leads to loss of the sales call.

In the second sentence, you didn't challenge what he said and didn't infer that the physician was lying either, but you respected his claim by noting if the side effects were reported again then you would report it, and at the same time you let the physician know that this side effect is not on the drug insert leaflet which contains information from the drug studies and research.

Handling objections

> *"An objection is not a rejection; it is*
> *simply a request for more information."*[8]
> *Bo Bennett*

Objections are a positive thing, and are indicative of positive interaction and interest. So, the first thing to remember is to stay calm, focused, and do not panic. Turn the negative into a positive by rephrasing the objection as a form of a positive question. This will help you to stay focused on answering the question instead of being stuck in the situation.

For example:

> CUSTOMER: "Your product is expensive."
> REPHRASE THE CUSTOMER'S OBJECTION IN YOUR MIND AS: "*Why* is your product more expensive than competing products?"

Another example:

> CUSTOMER: "We don't have enough money in our budget now."
> REPHRASE THE CUSTOMER'S OBJECTION IN YOUR MIND AS: "What am I going to do with my budget to be able to afford your product?"

Another example:

> DOCTOR: "My patients began to suffer from abdominal pain three days after starting to take this medication."
> REPHRASE THE CUSTOMER'S OBJECTION IN YOUR MIND AS: How am I going to deal with abdominal pain and is this a common side effect with all patients taking the medication?

Classifying objections by type

EASY OBJECTION. An objection that is based on a misunderstanding of some information.

DIFFICULT OBJECTION. An objection that is based on fact, such as a side effect or a high price or a precaution for your product.

FALSE OBJECTION. An objection that is based on making up false information mentioned by the customer to misdirect the sales rep. about your product. An objection can also be based on intentionally false information provided to the customer by a rep from a competing company, and the customer accepts it as valid and objects based on that invalid information.

Now you need to respond by the following CAAC (concede, ask, answer, confirm; as in the graphic below) Technique.

Step-by-step approach to handling objections:

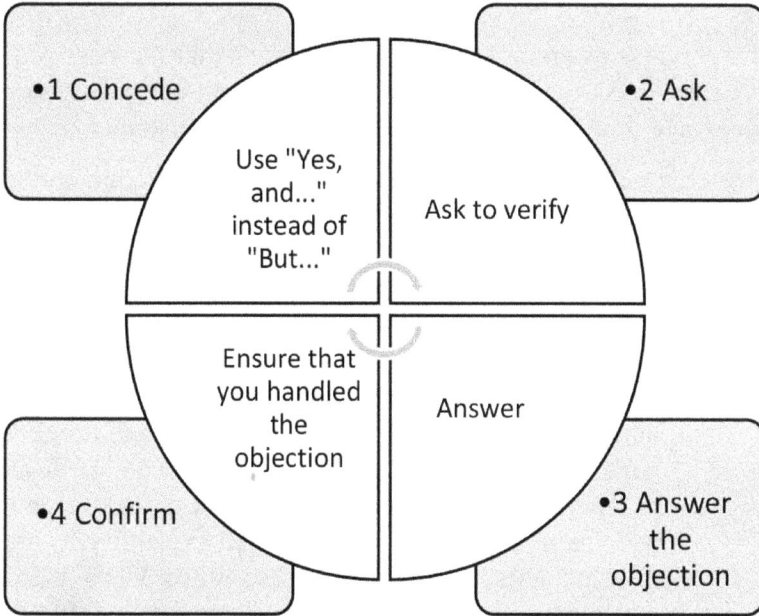

•1 Concede

Use "Yes, and..." instead of "But..."

•2 Ask

Ask to verify

Ensure that you handled the objection

Answer

•4 Confirm

•3 Answer the objection

Let's look at an example:

Dr. Expert: "My patients began to suffer from abdominal pain three days after starting to take this medication."

Take the objection in a form of question.

Rephrase the objection in your mind as: How am I going to address this abdominal pain and is this a common side effect with all patients taking the medication?

The CAAC Technique:

YOU SAY: *"(Concede)* Dr. Expert, I understand that some of your patients had abdominal pain three days from the start of the medication and would appreciate it if you would explore this further. *(Ask questions to clarify)* "How many patients suffered from abdominal discomfort out of the total number of patients treated?"

In patients who suffered from abdominal discomfort, had they taken the medication before or after their meals? For how long were they experiencing discomfort? How effective was the medication across all the patients you prescribed it to?

In the previous example I put all the questions that the sales professional should ask together, but in a real situation, you must ask one question at a time to avoid any confusion for your customer.

> DR. EXPERT: "Two patients in 30 had abdominal pain and they took the medication before meals. The pain was described as lasting for one hour and the efficacy was significant."
>
> SALES REP: *(Concede ")*As I understand that only 6% of your patients suffered from abdominal pain, is that correct?"
>
> DR. EXPERT: "Yes."
>
> SALES REP: *(Answering the objection)* "It's a good sign that the abdominal pain is not affecting large number of patients, however it's recommended that the medication be taken after meals and it's important to make sure that patients take it after they eat which explains why those three patients had abdominal discomfort. In the medication monograph it says that some patients might suffer from abdominal discomfort if they take the medication on an empty stomach, which could last from half an hour to an hour. The outcomes you mentioned were significant and match the expectation from the treatment.
>
> SALES REP: *(Confirm)* "Did I answer the question in the way you expect?"

Example of objection handling in medical device sales, based on one of my experiences.

I did a sales presentation about an operating room slush machine. An operating room slush machine velvety-textured appearance ice used in organ transplant surgeries to keep organs alive during the course of surgery until transplanted inside the body. I included all the steps needed to operate it. My customer liked the features and related outcomes and values compared to the competitor's machine which they had been using for 15 years. Obviously, it was old technology and it required someone to stand in front of the slush machine and scrape the ice buildup from the sides of the machine basin to prevent tissue damage during surgery. It also required an alcohol medium between the drape and the machine basin. My company's technology incorporated an automatic stir device which promoted the production of velvet slush ice so there was no need for anyone to stand in front of the machine to scrape the ice, no chance of sharp ice edges forming and building up and then causing tissue damage, and no need for an alcohol medium either, meaning that some significant hazards during surgery had been eliminated. The price difference between my product and the existing product was about $40,000.

Although the customer was amazed by the features and impacts, she still made an objection.

Here is the actual scenario:

> CUSTOMER: "The price is high, and we don't have enough money in our budget to buy your machine now."

In your mind, imagine the customer asked:
"Why is your price high and what am I going to do with my budget to be able to purchase your machine?

Second, classify the objection:
Is this a true (easy or difficult) objection, or a false objection?
   It's a true objection, because our product was more expensive.

Concede the facts:

> SALES REP: "I understand that there is a price difference and arranging budget could be challenging at this time of the year."

Here you acknowledged and emphasized understanding of your customer's objection which show respect for her position, which helps build rapport and prepares your customer to listen.

		Real objection like a side effect or high price
		Take the objection in a form of question.
Easy objection	Difficult objection	Apply CAAC objection handling
		Answer by minimizing the objection and break it down
		Mention each feature, impact, outcome and value
		Confirm
		Customer misunderstood any given information
		Take the objection in a form of question
		Apply CAAC objection handling
		Confirm

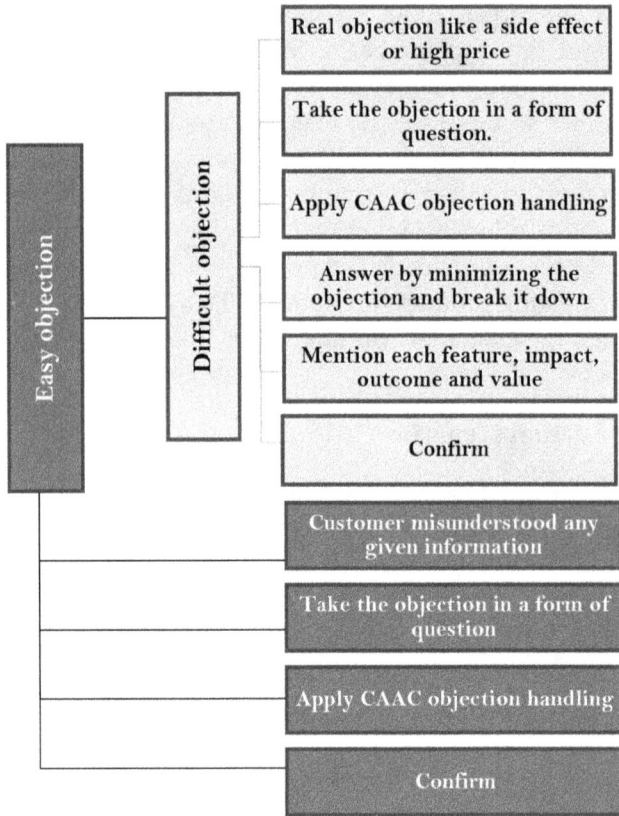

Remember: A problem's consequences
over time compel customers
to make an urgent change.

Ask to verify and mention her name.

> SALES REP: "Heather, how often do you do maintenance on the existing machines?" (They had two machines).
>
> CUSTOMER: "We have a maintenance contract in place."
>
> SALES REP: "How much roughly does it cost per machine and when does the contract start?"
>
> CUSTOMER: "Around 500 dollars a month and we have had the contract for 5 years now."

SALES REP: "So, you've paid around $30,000 for each machine in five years. Is that correct?"

CUSTOMER: "Yes."

SALES REP: "How many times per month, on average can you use the slush machines and what is the average time per surgery?"

CUSTOMER: "Twelve surgeries averaging five hours each."

SALES REP: "If we calculate the labor cost per use because of having one staff member scraping the ice for five hours, it comes to around 60 hours X $20 per hour = $1200 per month.

Answer the objection:

Pull out value technique:

SALES REP: "What would you think if we could remove the auto stir device and, in this situation, your staff will still need to stand in front of the machine and scrape the ice for the duration of the operation and might have sharp objects which could cause tissue damage that results in massive complications after surgery? This could save you up to $30,000, would you agree?" (The answer will be 'no.')

CUSTOMER: "I don't think this a good idea. What will be the benefit for the hospital if we get the same technology we have? Management will refuse for sure."

SALES REP: "Exactly, you are correct (support intervention). If management knew about the difference between the two technologies and how much our machine would improve patient outcomes and save money on staff and mainte-nance costs from having the auto stir device, they'd sit up and listen. From what you've told me, your budget was set 15 years ago when you bought your present machines. They need to be updated and our new technology will more than pay for itself." (This helps guide the customer in gaining approval on the budget).

Minimize the objection and break it down:

> SALES REP: *(A problem's consequences over time com-
> pel customers to make an urgent change)* "So, the
> machine you have costs $1200 labor + $500 maintenance =
> $1700 per month, totaling around $20,400 a year and in 5
> years it costs you $102,000 and for two machines $204,000.
> How does that sound to top management?"
>
> CUSTOMER: "I didn't realize that we pay that much." (Customer
> realizes how costly to maintain the machines).
>
> SALES REP: Definitely, yes, you are (support intervention). If I
> told you that we provide a warranty for the auto stir device
> for the life of the machine and you don't have to pay a sin-
> gle penny, saving $20,000 dollars a year by eliminating the
> labor and maintenance cost means saving $200,000 for the
> two machines in 5 years, how does that sound to you?"
>
> CUSTOMER: "Sounds great."
>
> SALES REP: "Absolutely, you are correct. We also offer a "try
> before you buy" program. I recommend that you try the
> machine first and do a demo for your staff to show that
> it makes velvet slush so it will not damage the organs. It
> will be safer for patients and it will prevent post-opera-
> tive complications. You'll also see how the auto stir device
> works to eliminate the need to scrape the ice which is very
> convenient for your staff since it will allow them to tend to
> other priorities in the operating room.

The customer requested a demo and trial. The most interesting part
happened during the demo, when, to my surprise, it was the operating
room manager - not me - who mentioned the features and outcomes
for her staff during the demo! This was a great buying signal, and they
placed an order for 3 machines.

7

The Complex Sales cycle

In the medical device sales field, sales are considered to be complex rather than simple sales calls so we call medical device sales a 'sales process'. Selling medical devices is complex especially in hospital settings. Your success very much depends on building the customer relationship and executing each step in the sales process, as all steps are linked to each other. Commitments gained at each step support commitments at the next step, which makes closing the sale easier and makes it all go more smoothly. The same applies for any sales process selling heavy equipment or high value products.

"Complex sales involve high value products and long sales cycles with multiple decision makers, and can refer to a process of buying used when procuring large contracts for supplies or services where the customer controls the buying process by issuing a Request for Proposal (RFP) and requires a proposal offer from previously identified or interested suppliers." ("What is Enterprise Sales and Why is it Important for Your Business?". Rachael Pilcher. *The Startup Finance Blog*. Lighter Capital. Retrieved 14 February 2019.)

There is a direct relationship between multiple decision makers involved and the level of risk that is involved in the purchase of supplies or services.

The sales process tends to be smooth transactional. If the purchase only impacts a small group of people or doesn't involve huge financial budget, then the decision could be made by one buyer.

If the purchase requests a huge financial allocation or can change the buyer's business model, then often more than one decision maker is involved in the buying process. In this kind of transaction, the sales person is required to have high executional skills.

If we consider imaging equipment, medical devices, implants or surgical equipment as examples of items included in a complex sale, the decision makers would primarily include physicians, the CFO, the CEO, admin, the radiology director, the director of surgical services, the materials management director, operating room director, director of imaging, director of IT while the top influencers would be physicians, the director of materials management and the director of surgical services.

There are two main triggers that initiate hospital equipment purchases:

- 70% of decision makers initiate purchasing decisions when replacing used or outdated technology.
- 40% of decision makers initiate purchasing decisions as a result of user requests.

While 7 out of 10 decision makers look to improve clinical outcomes when deciding to purchase, nearly 50% are looking for lower costs and 47% of purchases are made between 8 and 10 months.

That's why it's crucial to focus in your presentation on the clinical outcomes and values which make a difference between your solution and the existing one.

In contrast to complex sales, there is a simple sale or a sales situation which needs a one-to-one sales presentation and involves only one decision maker, so the sale will not be a complex sale, and its success depends on the decision of one buyer or one customer.

As mentioned previously, the sales process is not always a neat process. You might complete every step precisely and efficiently, but you still might get objections. You can't prevent customer objections at any step in the sales process. I consider objections a healthy situation because they indicate interest, as long as the objections seem reasonable. It's crucial to know how to handle them effectively and how to address customer concerns.

Eight Steps in Healthcare and Complex Sales Cycles

A healthcare (or other complex sales cycle) is composed of eight main steps. It can take from 3 to 12 months or longer to gain a commitment and include typically 6 to 8 calls for each product.

Here are the primary steps to follow:

1. Preparation for your sales call.
2. Uncover your customer's problem(s).
3. Presentation of your product and handling objections.
4. Demonstrate the product.
5. Trial.
6. Close the deal (secure a purchase order (P.O.)
7. Conduct an in-service.
8. Ask for referrals.

Step 1: Preparation

If we take an example in the medical device field as a part of healthcare sales, especially in hospital settings, preparation for sales resembles the process used for a pharmaceutical sales call, but it requires a few more steps to prepare for your sales call:

Know your customer

Take into consideration who is involved in the sales decision as it might be more than one person. It might be a buying decision that will be made by a committee, by influencers, and by an account purchasing department, or a GPO (group purchasing organization).

Gap analysis

Review the account's sales history, like customer relationship management (CRM), and do your gap analysis. Gap analysis involves the comparison of actual performance with potential or desired performance (usage gap = market potential – existing usage) and (product gap = the part of the market that you are missing because of your product outcomes). Review the account's sales history to determine what kind of products they are buying, how they are buying (direct purchase or through GPO), and if your product is going through contract and if so, the name of the contact person.

Review account website and investors section

Know your customer very well. If your customer has a website, be sure to read it. Determine all you can about the hospital's features, including the number of beds, what kind of services they offer, and how the hospital is managed. Review the website's investor information, if applicable.

Samples, Equipment, Literature

Prepare your bag. Include enough numbers of sales brochures, studies, and business cards. Samples from small disposables can be included for the intended department you are calling on (this is in case you are making a full sales call and the demo stage is included as well). Know who you are going to meet, what you are going to present, your sales strategy, your market segment, customer potential, and group purchasing organizations (GPO).

Setting an appointment:

One of the challenges facing sales professionals is making an appointment. Call your customer first to make the appointment. If this doesn't work, then the most effective way is to send her/him an *outlook invitation* with two dates and time options and include a brief and focused note stating the purpose of the meeting and the agenda, and indicating how what you have to offer will benefit the customer's practice. Usually specify 30 minutes for the meeting. This technique works perfectly.

I will give a great example of this approach working well. I was trying to make an appointment with the OR manager at one of the major hospitals in Winnipeg, but she was very busy. I was trying to make an appointment using all methods like phone calls, emails, leaving a message on her voice mail but received no replies.

I decided to send her an outlook invite and specified two dates and times and specified in the body of the *invite* (*"Introducing our new fluid warmer, please accept any one of the invitations if the time and date are convenient for you"*).

I received a response to my invitation within two hours. She accepted one of the dates and I was able to sell the fluid warmer to her.

What happened here? Most of the decision makers don't have time to reply to emails or phone calls. They see this like a cold call, like the phone calls we receive at home from companies wanting to sell us some item or service that we have no need or interest in. To them it's a waste of their time.

TO SET A SUCCESSFUL APPOINTMENT, SEND AN MS OUTLOOK INVITATION WITH TWO OPTIONS FOR DATE AND TIME

By sending an MS Outlook invite, you show that your time is valuable as well as their time, and once you specify the time frame for the meeting and agenda, then they become very interested and they will appreciate your time, by doing so, they would know the topic of discussion, the value they could get from the meeting, and how much time they should set aside, on the top of that, no more actions required as the outlook invite will pop-up in their calendar.

I used the same method with most of my difficult- to-see customers and have been very successful at a rate of 90%. I shared the idea with the team, and they were successful in setting appointments with their difficult-to-see customers. The most preferred appointment time is just prior to or just after lunch time so, 11:00 am or 1:00 pm unless specified differently by the customer when he/she replies to your outlook invite. You need to be very focused in your message. Introduce yourself and express appreciation for their time in setting up a meeting to discuss specific solutions from which they would benefit.

Example:

> Hi Sally,
> This is Mark from (your company name), your Area Territory Manager for Hypothermia solutions.
>
> *Meeting Agenda*
>
> (*A strong value statement*) I really appreciate you sharing 30 minutes of your time to discuss an innovative solution which has helped many customers improve patient outcomes and reduce operating room costs.
>
> *Area of discussion*
>
> Controlling patient hypothermia at the point of use (in the operating room). I'd appreciate it if you can choose any day and time from the invitation I sent that works best for you. If the date and time are not suitable, simply change them to suit your schedule and send it back. Please let me know if you have any questions.
>
> Have a great day
> Warm regards
> Mark
> Tel: xxx-xxx-xxxx

This is an example of how to set an appointment with a well-defined potential customer in your existing area, for example, if you have been successful in getting an email for your potential customer or key decision maker. You have also already done your search and you already know that your solution has more value compared with what they are using.

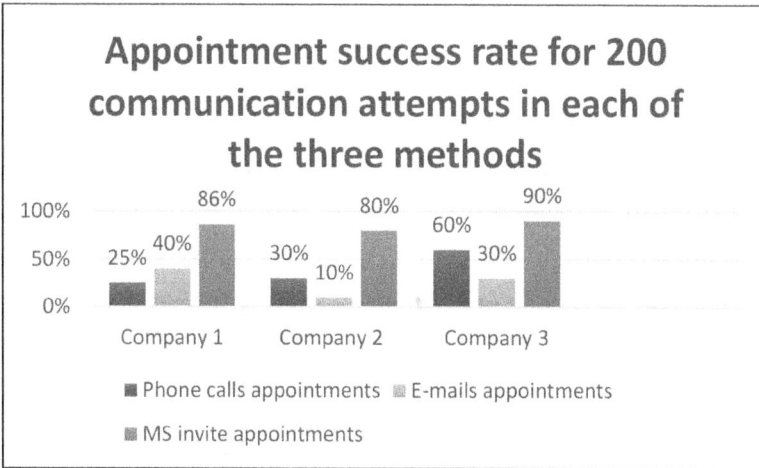

Appointment success rate for 200 communication attempts in each of the three methods

In the previous illustration, a study shows the appointment success rate for 300 calls in each multinational company, divided into 100 phone calls, 100 emails and 100 MS outlook invitation in an attempt to secure an appointment.

In the first multinational chemical company for Healthcare, appointment success rate was 86% using MS invite, in the second large laboratory group, appointment success rate was 80% using MS invite and in the third largest pharmaceutical distributor, appointment success rate was 90% using MS invite.

If you have been successful to make a phone call and get your prospect over the phone to secure an appointment, it's important to send an invite following the phone call so your prospect will remember the topic of discussion, and the time needed for the meeting.

The number of appointments you already secured is directly related to the number of opportunities in your pipeline: the more opportunities you get the more chances you have to close deals.

Important tips:

The main goal of sending an MS outlook invitation is to secure an appointment with the difficult-to-visit customers, not to try to sell anything. Try to make the appointment using a phone call or email first. If this fails, try the MS outlook invite. Don't send MS outlook invites to prospects randomly without doing a preparation step in advance, which includes your search about that prospect, getting their email, etc.

Your message must be concise, clear and to the point of interest and must include the following:

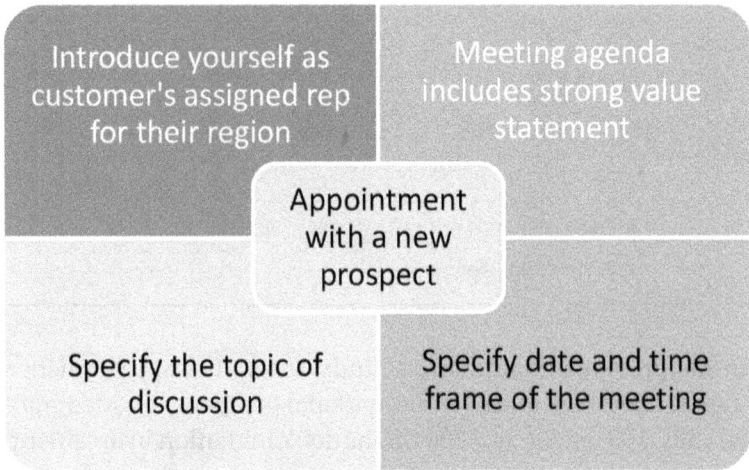

Introduce yourself as customer's assigned rep for their region	Meeting agenda includes strong value statement
Specify the topic of discussion	Specify date and time frame of the meeting

Appointment with a new prospect

Questions you should ask and answer yourself in step 1. These questions and your prepared answers will help you to build your strategy to prepare and present your product efficiently and ultimately lead to a demo, a product trial and then the closing of the sale.

About your product

1. Does your product offer an added value to the customer compared to what the customer is currently using?
2. How superior is the value of your product compared with what the customer is presently using? How important is the new solution to the customer's practice?
3. How easy is it to implement the new solution compared with the solution presently in use by your customer?

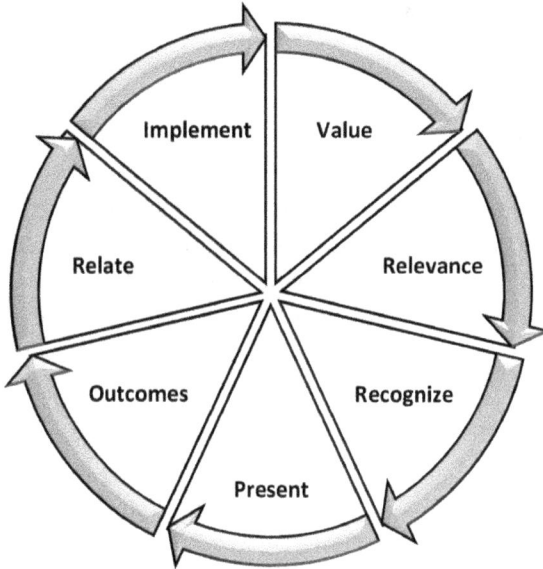

About product/customer wish relationship

1. How will you lead your customers to recognize their clinical needs or wishes and how they are solved thanks to your product's added value?
2. How will you present your value?
3. How will you relate your product's value to your customer's wishes or needs?
4. How will you show the impact of an added feature on your customer's daily practice?
5. How will you simplify the implementation of the new solution?

Prospecting and qualifying

Remember setting an appointment with an already known potential customer is different from setting an appointment with a totally new prospect. In the previous situation, you already knew your prospect and you knew that he/she is your potential customer or is a key decision- maker.

Prospecting is the process of finding potential customers. These are customers you did not previously know about.

Prospecting for a totally new area

Prospecting starts by defining your target market segment, and defining potential accounts into this market segment according to the prospect's buying power, size, and annual revenues. Prospecting priority might be given to accounts receiving open budget of funds from the government or according to the account potential in the private sector. Hospitals vary in the amount of funding available to them, with some hospitals, such as those that receive a lot of charitable donations, being particularly good prospects to a pharmaceutical or medical device sales rep.

Preparation for prospecting

You need to define your message's goal in the preparation step for prospecting, whether your message will be delivered over the phone or in a personal meeting.

In the preparation step of prospecting, you need to review the account, identify what problems they might have and how your solution could solve their problem's impacts and related outcomes. To obtain this information, you need to do an Internet search for the prospect's account. Study the board of directors, identify key leaders, read the mission statement, and review the balance sheet and the size of the account.

To better identify the issues that the prospect might have, read their transparency and compliance report which may be on their site or published on the health authority's site.

When I was working as an account executive for a multinational company that manufactured infection control products, I was selling a solution to minimize healthcare-associated infections. The transparency and compliance report described the incidence rates of C. diff (clostridium difficile) and MRSA (Methicillin Resistant Staphylococcus Aureus) in each hospital in my territory. Since I could then identify the hospitals that had the highest incidence of C.diff and MRSA, I prepared the TPM (tailored prospecting message) tailored to each account's situation and was able to sell our solution to those hospitals.

YOUR FOCUS WHEN YOU MEET WITH YOUR
PROSPECTS IS TO IDENTIFY THEIR CHALLENGES
AND BUILD RAPPORT

Prospecting process in a totally new area

Tailored Prospecting message (TPM)

You need to be prepared with a unique, scripted message tailored to fit the prospect you are calling on when you meet with him/her or speak over the phone (in the case of inside sales professionals).

Don't pick up the phone and call the prospect without preparing a *TPM (Tailored prospecting message).*

TPMs include an introduction that describes your company, summarize the kind of solutions your company offers for this specific prospect based on your research in the preparation for this call. Don't mention the names of the products yet; instead, focus on the problem's impact and most importantly its related outcomes (if you have successfully determined the problem in advance). Have your pinpoint questions ready so that you can determine what the prospect's problems and needs are, and how much potential this customer might have.

Establish a contact list

Identify key opinion leaders (KOL) or decision-making persons and influencers as well.

You might need to make a visit to the prospect's facility to gather information from the information office or desk. Find out who the best contact person(s) is/are. You might also be able to gather this information by making a phone call prior to making an appointment.

In some situations, the information office will advise you how to contact the prospect, which could be through the prospect's administrative assistant. You might be able to meet him/her directly to introduce yourself and ask for an appointment. Don't ask for an appointment for the next day, for example. You want to have time to gather more information about your prospect, and to prepare for your qualifying and sales call process. If you met with the secretary, you need to gather information such as their email and phone numbers (which could be direct phone number or a general phone number with an extension).

Making an appointment with a new prospect

Before any prospect agrees to meet with you, (s)he has important questions in mind that led to agreeing to meet with you:

- What are you going to talk about? Are you going to speak about something which they know already, or will you talk about something new?
- Is it worth their time to meet with you? What's in it for them? Are you going to provide them with great value that could positively impact their practice?
- How much time do they need to set aside for this meeting?

If you want to be successful making your appointment, then you need to answer those questions in your message when you ask for an appointment.

Your first priority during your initial contact is to make an appointment. Avoid trying to qualify a prospect over the phone. You need to have a face-to-face meeting to see their body language, facial expressions and eye contact. This job can be harder for inside sales professionals who depend mainly on the prospect's vocal tone, pauses and reactions as well as the way they answer questions.

In some other situations, the prospect's office manager might give you an email address for the prospect. This will be a great opportunity to send him/her an MS Outlook invitation so that you can secure an appointment.

Meeting your prospect

Your goal in the first meeting (prospecting meeting) is to gather information, learn about your customer's practice, identify issues and problem, and then go back to Step 1: Preparation, before making any sales call. In most of the cases, if your prospect agrees to make an appointment, then there is a higher chance that you will sell your product.

When you call a prospect or send an email or ask for a meeting, you need to know your goal and what are you going to say, how you are going to express it and how you would start your conversation. Be prepared with your TPM (tailored prospecting message).

Some trainers ask you to qualify the prospect financially first: if their budget won't allow for them to buy anything from you, then don't waste any more time on that prospect. My advice *to you is to refrain from asking this kind of question in your first meeting*, because if you have the right solution for a problem's impact, then customer can allocate the budget to purchase your solution or can create the budget for it. If you have successfully shown your solution's value, then prospects can arrange for the budget. They might not have the budget right away, but they can arrange for it in the new years' budget. In my experience, qualifying a prospect starts with defining the customer's problems first rather than whether the prospect's budget presently allows for an immediate purchase.

If you asked the customer, "do you have room in your budget?" in the very early stage of the sales process without having first built rapport, the automatic answer would be NO. Remember customers are emotionally entangled with their problems, and the customer considers any change as a big hassle as they need to do lot of requests, follow ups, answer questions from top management, obtain signatures, send info for committee reviews and approval, etc. So, when you ask the customer in the first meeting of the sales process if they have funds or not, if they think it'll be hard to get approval for purchases, they'll immediately just give up on the idea of considering your product.

Once you have identified potential prospects, then those prospects must be considered a top priority for making a professional sales call.

Relationship and building Rapport with potential prospects

In Step 1: Preparation, you should meet with all persons involved, like all decision makers, some of whom may be the head of department, the department manager, departmental clinical coordinators and educators, head nurse, purchasing managers, and GPO personnel.

You should build the relationship first. Make at least two visits to your customer before you start selling a product. By the end of the second visit, ask about the relationship with your company. For example: *"How would you describe your relationship with our company so far?"*

If you try to sell to this account before making this step and the customer had a previous issue with your company, then you will end up with sales failure. You might be surprised to learn that some customers complain about a situation that happened in the past which caused them to stop buying from your company. The first thing you should do in this situation is to resolve the issue and clarify it.

Here's a list of the important steps you need to follow.

Do your homework:

1. How does the customer's department operate?
2. How does your product fit into this department?
3. How does your product work?
4. How could your product solve a customer's problems through its features, impacts, outcomes and values?
5. What they are using right now?
6. How do your competitor's products work? What are their weakness and strengths?
7. Who is involved in the buying decision?
8. Who are the key players?
9. Who could be your champion?
10. How does the buying process work here?

QUALIFYING PROSPECTS

∞ Don't ask about budget in the first meeting.
∞ Your goal in the first meeting is to gather information.
∞ Understand customer practices. It may take another meeting spent observing in customer's practice to fully understand how it is functioning.
∞ Which product(s) is/are currently in use?
∞ What is the current level of satisfaction?
∞ Identify problems.
∞ Uncover the needs or wishes.
∞ Who else is involved in the buying decision?
∞ If the customer is interested, how soon can they buy?
∞ How does the buying process work there?
∞ Qualifying may take more than one meeting.

Example:

If you get hired to sell a line of products that are new to you, like selling detergents to CSSD unit (central sterile services department), it's very crucial to learn how your customer's department operates. You can ask the customer for more information about their practice, *get permission to spend some time* in the department to learn about the equipment they use and how they clean it; observe what kind of products they are using and how they use them; take a look inside their machines and see if there are stains building up inside their sterilizers (which would be indicative of hard water including metals). Always look for the issues they face and take note of the possible issues they might have, as this will help you to prepare for your sales call and offer the best solutions, create an extra valued impact and outcome compared with what they are using (wish creation).

Trusted partner and advisor role:

Sometimes customers realize that they have an issue but don't know how it occurred or how to solve it. Sometimes, they don't realize that there are issues in their practice, and sometimes they don't know what they really need. Being in the customer's practice for some time will help you as a problem solver or as a solution ambassador, to identify the issues or the challenges, give you the opportunity to offer the best solution, and act as a consultative sales professional and trusted partner instead of just selling a product.

In one of the multinational medical device companies I was working for as a territory manager, we had a product in our company portfolio in the form of a solid, odorless block to clean sterilizers. This solid block cleaner was to be placed inside the sterilizer and with just one cycle of cleaning, the sterilizer would be left shining. My client was using a liquid chemical cleaner which had a strong smell. How did I know this? Well, I had asked my customer's permission to stay for an hour in their CSSD unit learning how the cleaning process worked there.

My customer was not aware that there were issues. They were actually happy with their current product. During my one-hour stay in the CSSD, I saw two of the staff dealing with the chemical wearing PPE (personal protective equipment) which is a must-use in this department, but they were coughing. In addition, the cleaner came in big drums: drums ready for use, drums in use, and empty drums, all of which took up a huge amount of storage space.

I also noted that staff members were using a liquid instrument cleaner which had a strong smell. That cleaner was used to prepare the instrument before the main cleaning process began. In our portfolio, we had an instrument cleaner that was odorless and foamy.

I appreciated my customer's time allowing me to stay for one hour inside their department to learn about their practice, but I didn't do a sales call that day.

I left their facility and wrote down the issues they had, such as:

Problem: using liquid chemicals to clean the sterilizer and instruments. The problem's impact and related outcomes:

- Splashing can be a chemical hazard and have related costs.
- The odor would irritate the staff causing coughing and related treatment costs.
- Precautions had to be taken handling and transporting the chemical thus increasing their costs.
- Bulk storage for the drums was an obvious added cost.

A brief example of applying the APWS Selling Method for the previous situation:

After I went home, I prepared to do a sales call by doing the following:

Step 1. Prepare

I created a PowerPoint presentation for the customer. Just one slide for the attention grabber, one slide about awareness for the existing problem impacts, one slide about awareness for the best solution, its outcomes and values and two to three slides for Step 3 which is a presentation about the product.

Prepared the pinpoint question model to create the wish or need and engage the customer in a constructive discussion.

I also focused on meeting with all decision makers separately (could be one or a maximum of two decision makers at a time). Remember that meeting with them separately is intended to avoid encountering unwanted behavior which could be worsened in a group setting. The advantage would be that it would be easier to handle any objections (handling one person's objection is better than handling four or five people's objections at the same time), it would reduce the chance of encountering rejection behavior in a group meeting and, it gives you more control of the sales call.

I focused on getting one or two decision makers to become champions of my solution.

The Awareness process:

Let's talk about the most important part here which is the awareness process in pharmaceuticals which I recommend be included in the attention grabber statements as the customer doesn't have enough time to separate attention grabber from the awareness process. In a complex sale in any sales field, it's recommended that the Awareness process be done after the attention grabber and in conjunction with the Uncover stage, as doing so will give you the opportunity to strengthen this important stage and ultimately prepare your customer for accepting your solution.

More than 50% of your sales call success depends upon executing the awareness process along with the uncover stage.

In the awareness process, there are three parts. First, you make your customer aware of the existing problem's impacts (which has been discovered either during your visit or when the customer walks you through their process). Second, you make your customer aware of a better solution for those problems. Third, let your customer know that there are other accounts that have started using the new solution and that the new solution has solved exactly the same problems as the present customer has, which can make the customer realize that he or she needs to reassess the product in use and compel him or her to take action.

In the previous example:

(A) *Awareness about an existing problem's impacts and related outcomes:*

Plan to increase awareness about the existing problems like hazards from splashing chemicals, allergic reactions and health problems which might arise and persist from long-term inhaling chemical odors and related costs; handling and transportation precautions, and storage-related costs. Increasing awareness about an existing problem will help your prospects realize the problems they have.

(B) Awareness about a better solution:

Increase awareness about the solution, and how this solution solved similar problems for different accounts. We mention each problem, its impacts and outcomes on the customer's practice and how to solve each one. Again, you are not talking yet about your product, here you are talking about a solution without mentioning your product's name.

Doing so has great advantages: it gives every staff member the chance to comprehend the problem and let them wish there was a better solution. Staff members can discuss this matter and spread the word that something better is available

In the Awareness stage, you are not presenting your product yet, but we are talking about the proposed solution, so don't jump to your product until the Present stage. It's an important preparatory step for step 3 which is the Present step for the product.

Once you have completed the awareness steps, then you need to ask pinpoint questions that will serve to create or identify what your customer's needs or wishes are.

> *In the uncover step, be ready to ask your customer the pinpoint questions, as mentioned before, that some customers don't realize what kind of problems they might have.*

Present stage (will be explained in detail)

Prepare for the solution, set its features, impacts, outcomes, and values, and prepare for any objections and prepare for their answers.

1. Lead the customer toward asking for a demo.
2. Conduct a product trial.
3. Ask for the P.O. (purchase order).
4. In-service. Implementation
5. Ask for referrals

I followed these steps exactly and I got the P.O.

Another example:

If you get hired to sell laparoscopic instruments and equipment for the first time, ask permission to attend one or two surgeries before selling. This will help you understand how surgeons conduct the operations and what they are using. Then you will have a better idea about their practice and how your solution differs from what they are presently using.

If you are introducing a new product to an existing client with whom you have a relationship already, then your job should be easier. In your following visit, again, your first focus before starting to sell the solution is to increase awareness about an existing problem which might be common with different clients. This will arouse interest and prepare your client to hear about the solution.

Let's go through in detail for Step 2: Uncover needs and wishes (asking questions).

Step 2: Uncover stage

Let's talk about the second stage in your actual sales call, it's the most important step for your sales call success, prior to this stage, you already built a case, setting your call opening, used an attention grabber, increased awareness about an existing problem and awareness about a solution which helped similar accounts to solve the same problems.

In the uncover stage, you prepare your questions in order to target existing weaknesses that you can assist the customer in eliminating.

Use your listening skills to ensure you capture what is said and not said. Ensure that you understand the customer and know your sales call objective. This is an active process stage of identifying gaps with your customer and securing their agreement to proceed.

Scenario

You are a selling minimally-invasive system to determine cardiac hemodynamic functions, which doesn't need a catheter insertion through the femoral artery. Instead of the catheter, a sensor can be hooked to one side of a cardiac monitor and the other sensor side is hooked onto the patient's finger by a clip and connected to an existing pressure line. The sensor transmits signals from patient's finger which are interpreted into numbers on the cardiac monitor.

Customer you are calling on:

You are calling on the chief anesthesiologist in a famous liver transplant hospital who is using an invasive technique of catheter insertion to monitor cardiac hemodynamics.

Call opening and attention grabber:

> SALES REP: *"In your practice, you see patients in need of liver transplants. Monitors for cardiac hemodynamics during surgery are very crucial especially in this long surgical procedure. Using an invasive pulmonary artery wedge pressure catheter could cause trauma and might increase surgical site infections and post-op complications. Obviously, it's preferable to reduce surgical site infections, reduce the length of hospital stays and reduce postoperative costs instead."*

Or you can use another pitch such as:

> SALES REP: *"Mr. Chris, I am here today to offer a great solution which has helped more than 15 hospitals reduce intraoperative and post-operative costs and this is achieved by reducing surgical site infections by 99.9% which reduces the associated costs of infections."*

In this pitch, you start with a value statement by stating the impact on the customer's practice and the outcomes for the patients and the practice.

This example illustrates selling minimally-invasive cardiac output monitors for the anesthesia department. Such devices monitor heart function during anesthesia. You need to increase awareness about the difficulty that all anesthesiologists face during surgery while monitoring heart function, such as difficulty inserting catheters, complications arising from invasive procedures (e.g., infections, perforations), missing heart function data on the cardiac monitor, difficult-to-use software. Is their current product invasive or non-invasive, what does the customer use right now? What does the competitor's software look like? Find out what really bothers them using their existing procedures and equipment.

Then ask the customer to walk you through their existing procedure. Let them explain to you how they do it, and encourage them to elaborate about what they wish would be different so that they would be free of these problems.

Another example:

You are selling detergents for surgical instruments in the central reprocessing department. Focus on the difficulties facing staff when they perform the cleaning process for surgical instruments. This could include splashing chemicals, corrosive detergent action on the instruments, and detergent smells which irritate the staff. Ask about effective instrument cleaning when a detergent lacks sufficient enzymes, a problem which could negatively affect the cleaning process in different surgical procedures.

Ask customers to walk you through their instrument cleaning process starting from the operating room right up to and including packing the instruments to be ready for surgical use. During the discussion focus on recording the problems that the staff could face in each step of the cleaning procedure. Ask open-ended questions for best results.

Customer: Problem bond

On many occasions, sales professionals face a situation in which they did everything right, but the customer doesn't want to stop using the product he or she has been using.

In this case, the customer gets used to seeing or experiencing the problem every day. As time passes, the problem becomes a habit or daily reality and the bond between the problem and the customer become stronger.

When the sales professional offers a new solution that would be much more convenient, (s)he could still face rejection simply because the customer has a strong bond with the existing problem.

For example, in the past, customers were using intermittent catheterization to determine the post-void residual in the urinary bladder. When bladder scans were first introduced to the market to determine PVR (post-void residual) invasively, the process faced lot of rejection. Urologists and other HCPs (healthcare professionals) didn't accept the change easily from intermittent catheterization to the non-invasive technique using the bladder scan, a procedure which was more convenient for the patient and for the staff, and which reduced urinary tract infections (UTIs) and the cost of related treatment which resulted from the invasive technique (the problem).

Why did these rejections happen? Simply because HCPs got used to the invasive technique, and as time passed, this technique became part of their daily practice. The bond between the invasive technique and HCPs strengthened and came to be a protocol that needed to be followed by all staff members.

THE KEY TO BREAKING THE CUSTOMER : PROBLEM BOND IS TO GET A PRODUCT TRIAL AND INCREASE A TRIAL'S DURATION.

How can you break the bond between the problem and the customer so that the HCPs are open to accepting a new and more convenient solution?

1. Increase the HCPs' awareness of the problem by explaining how the problem has affected other HCPs at other medical facilities.
2. Increase awareness about a better solution, its positive impact and superior outcomes.
3. Give an example from a strong reference who is using the new solution and how it solved lot of problems.
4. Ask for a product trial. This essential for breaking the bond with the existing product that was in use.
5. Increase the duration of the trial period to create a customer bond with the new solution. This is essential for creating a new bond to your product.

Role of the Internet in buying decisions

There has been a huge shift in buyers' attitudes towards the buying process, especially since funding for attendance at conferences and trade shows has become limited and there are greater time pressure constraints. Your customers can access all the information online that they need - morning, noon and night.

Over half of hospitals and healthcare facilities, and manufacturer's administrators go online to research equipment and vendors. They usually identify vendors and compare products by gathering information from different resources through search engines, and they look for product features and functionality by searching for videos. They can ask sales professionals who have a good relationship with them, or seek information from professional societies, peers and sometimes conferences.

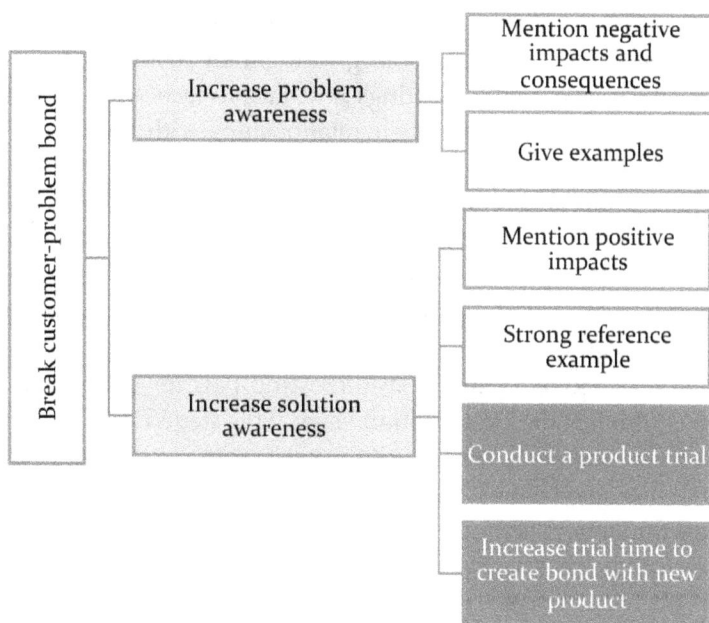

The primary reason buyers use search engines is to limit the number of vendors and around 80% of buyers and administrators contact a vendor as a result of their search.

Most buyers go online and read product reviews and read peer testimonials.

Be prepared during your sales meeting with a customer to be honest in the information you provide as some buyers validate what you are saying by performing online searches *during* the meeting.

Product videos and demos drive buyers to take action. Online videos help buyers decide if they want to get in front of a sales person or not.

Just as you prepare for a sales meeting with a buyer, buyers will prepare themselves too. Online research gives the buyers the knowledge to ask you the right questions.

There is a dual role of sales professionals and their vendor's marketing departments to increase their chances for selling, and the corner stone is relationship building. Sales professionals need to register themselves in professional societies, and continue to attend the meetings, as doing so will help sales professionals stay up to date about trends and new regulations in their field, and give them an advantage over competitors. Being present at meetings and face-to-face with buyers and decision makers strengthens their relationships with them and helps increase the chance that they would be the first contact for requests later.

Vendors' marketing departments need to help potential customers find the vendor's products by ensuring that their online content is search engine optimized (SEO) and fully viewable/accessible on tablets and mobile screens. Marketing departments must be sure to upload demo videos wherever possible.

Now let's move to the most interesting part for every sales professional which is the Presentation stage. This stage is the favorite for sales reps because they consider it the easiest step in the sales process. In fact, it needs to be mastered professionally. In the following section, you will find a new technique for presenting your product which will help in closing more sales.

Important definitions relevant to the Presentation stage

- **Benefit**
  "Something that produces good or helpful results or effects or that promotes well-being."[9]

- **Impact of a new intervention**
  Assesses the changes attributable to a particular intervention, and "this involves a counterfactual analysis, that is, a comparison between what actually happened and what would have happened in the absence of the intervention. Impact evaluation helps people answer key questions for evidence-based policy making: what works, what doesn't, where, why and for how much."[10]
- **Impact of an existing problem**
  Assesses the changes attributable to a particular problem, a comparison between what actually happened and what would have happened in the absence of the problem.
- **Outcome of a new intervention**
  It's the probability of a possible result of a new solution or intervention, which examines whether targets have been achieved.
- **Outcomes of problem's impacts**
  It's the potential adverse effects resulting from a problem's impact going unresolved over the course of weeks, months, or even years, and which can result in significant harm/damage.
- **Value:**
  "Denotes the degree of importance of some thing or action, or to describe the significance of different action."[11]

Step 3: The Presentation Stage:

FIOV presentation model (Feature/Impact/Outcome/Value)

Every time you sell a product, it's a chance to implement a new or different intervention. Every intervention must have impacts, outcomes and values to be considered for implementation. In the past, we used to say 'sell the features' benefits. 'Benefit' is such a general word. Some sales professionals refer the word 'benefit' to the outcomes, and some refer it to impacts, and some relate it to values. This created different approaches and explanations for the word 'benefit' and as a result, in many situations, the customer wasn't able to make a buying decision because, quite simply, (s)he didn't grasp the real meaning behind the word.

FIOV presentation model
(Feature-Impact-Outcome-Value)

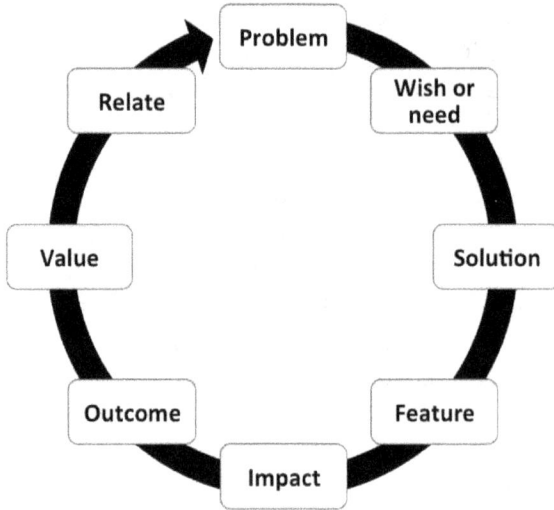

- Every customer has a wish to solve a problem
- Every product has a feature
- Every Feature has an impact
- Every Impact has an outcome
- Every outcome has a value
- Every value solves a problem

Example: Selling a detergent which has a neutral PH for surgical instrument cleaning.

Let's first consider what the problem is and what its impact might be. Always focus on the impact of the problem rather than just the problem itself. Focusing on the problem without highlighting the impacts leaves customers unable to recognize what they are really facing. Every problem has impacts and related outcomes which may result in harm and perhaps even cause severe damage. Mentioning the problem's impacts without mentioning the related outcomes will

only provide the customer with half the information that is required to understand the main issue.

It's not uncommon for sales professionals to focus on the problem while failing to pay attention to what would happen if the problem continues. (related problem impact's outcomes)

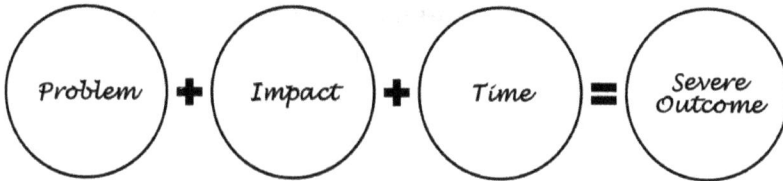

The longer a problem's consequences (such as severe harm and damage) are left to persist unresolved, the greater the potential damage there is to equipment and to patients/users or to customer's practice. For example, if surgical instruments are coming out of the cleaning process less than 100% clean, and the problem persists for one year, the harm and damage would be much more severe and more widespread than if the problem had been resolved a month after the problem developed. In medical settings, this could mean that more patients developed avoidable/preventable infections and higher healthcare costs related to re-cleaning or replacing instruments, and treating patient for those infections could have been avoided.

The key is not only to identify the problems but to alert your customer to the consequences of letting the problem persist for a long time. The customer will then realize that an immediate change is required. Urgency is the key to creating a change, whether it's a change in customer behavior or a change in the product used by the customer.

Problem intervention time:

You could intervene at the customer's facility, factory or jobsite when the problem first appears, or you could intervene when the problem has already started to bring added consequences, or you could intervene when the problem is severe. The first people to become aware of the problem are not the managers but staff members, followed by supervisors and then later, by management.

That's why it's important to have relationships not only with decision makers but also with staff members. Managers get involved when an issue becomes significant and then they start to look for the solution.

Building a relationship with everyone in the customer's practice/workplace (especially supervisors) helps you identify problems sooner and gives you the opportunity to offer your solutions to save the facility extra costs that would be incurred if the problem is allowed to persist over time. In many situations, staff members or supervisors will advise you how to open the discussion about the problem with their managers, and will define the consequences of the problem that are affecting them.

The key in any sale is to build trust and confidence with your customer. No manager would tell you about the problems they have upon first meeting him or her, even if you were the most talented person in identifying problems. On the contrary, managers and decision makers are highly reluctant to acknowledge that their departments have any problems, but once they trust you, they usually open up and reveal the issues adversely affecting their departments.

As mentioned before, to earn trust and confidence means you are asking your customer's permission to understand their practice which can include asking permission to spend some time in their department. This will give you the chance to be face-to-face with staff members and supervisors and to learn about their issues, some of which they might not realize they have, or some of which may just be developing.

Since managers solicit their staff's opinions about new solutions and how convenient they are for the staff, being on-site to observe what is happening will strengthen your relationship with everyone at that jobsite.

FIOV presentation model:

Your first step before presenting your product's features is to let your customer come to the realization that (s)he is at risk of value loss and unnecessary costs if they don't use your product or solution.

Your focus is to offer a solution to alleviate the problem's impact and their outcomes that an existing problem is having.

Problem: Using acidic or alkaline instrument cleaners.

What are the problem impacts and outcomes on the customer's practice as a result of using acidic or alkaline detergents?

- Stain build-up on the instruments. (problem impact)
- Corrosive action. (problem Impact)
- Reduction in instrument life. (problem outcome with continued use)
- High instrument replacement cost. (problem outcome with continued use)
- Increased cost of cleaning by adding neutralizers to remove the stains. (problem outcome increases the longer the product is used)
- The cost of cleaning, for example: how much would the customer have paid or saved if this outcome continued for two years versus two months?
- You need to mention the cost savings to your customer and how much (s)he would pay in each case.
- Increased cost of maintenance for sterilizers due to buildup of stains. (problem outcome gets worse the longer the product is used)

In this situation you are implementing a new solution for an intervention to clean surgical instruments. Let's see how to present your product's feature to your customer.

- **Feature:**
  The solution is a neutral PH.
- **Feature's Impact:**
  To assess the impact on the instrument, you need to ask yourself: what effect would using a neutral PH detergent have on the instrument?

  The impact of having a neutral PH feature on the instrument would be the prevention of the corrosive action on the instrument, in contrast to what would happen if alkaline or acidic cleaners were used.

- **Impact's Outcome:**

  What is the possible result of preventing the corrosive action?

  Answer: longer instrument life.

- **Outcome's Value:**

  How important is it to have longer instrument life?

  Value: Reduce instrument replacement costs and the costs to the hospital overall.

  In the present stage, it's important to mention the feature, its impacts, outcomes and values.

  As you can see here the word 'benefits' was not defined, but it could be one of them or could be all of them.

How to present this feature to your customer:

> SALES REP: *"It has a neutral PH, so it prevents the corrosive action on the instrument, and as a result it extends instrument life and reduces instrument replacement costs and the hospital's costs overall."*

Mentioning the values without mentioning the impacts and outcomes doesn't mean anything; it's like a chain, in that if you removed one part, it will be disconnected.

Example: cardiac output monitors with minimally invasive technique. Let's see how the Uncover and Present stage might look:

Here are some examples of questions you should ask that will help your customers better understand their wishes. Remember to be creative and focused in your questions.

1. "If you were the marketing manager for your company's existing product, what would you like to see changed on your cardiac output monitor?"
2. "What are the most important criteria you are looking for in a new cardiac output monitor?"
3. "How you distinguish which of two cardiac output monitors is superior?"
4. "If you had to choose between two cardiac monitors, what would influence your choice of one of them over the other one?"
5. "What do a new product's impacts and outcomes need to be for you to consider the new product superior to what you are presently using to reduce surgical site infections?"

6. "If you had a choice between using an invasive or a minimally invasive technique, which would be safer and minimize surgical site infections? Or which one would you prefer?"

First you identify the problems, the problem's impacts and related outcomes, and then you work on converting customer wishes/needs by pointing out real solutions that result from your product's features, impacts, outcomes and values.

Note: Please remember all the previous questions related to the existing competitor's product and try to identify an existing product impact's gap. It all represents *wish*-creating questions.

CUSTOMER: "I would prefer to use an invasive technique as I am used to it and it provides more accurate results." *The problem here is that there is a customer bond with an inferior product or process.*

SALES REP: *(Show empathy)* "I understand." *(The way to create a wish)*, "In your experience, what are the most common complications you've faced using invasive techniques?"

CUSTOMER: "Mostly surgical site infections but we give extensive courses of antibiotics and the patients will be fine." *The customer doesn't yet recognize that there is a problem because they are so accustomed to dealing with the problem.*

SALES REP: "That's exactly what the other accounts facing, surgical site infections are one of the biggest challenges, customers always look for better outcomes in that situation." *(Awareness about common existing problem with the other similar accounts and support intervention)*.

SALES REP: "How does this impact the post-operative costs?" This *leads to realization of problem's impact.*

CUSTOMER: "About $300 per patient." *Now the customer should start to realize that there is a problem.*

SALES REP: "How many patients going under surgery per week?"

CUSTOMER: "Eight patients in average."

SALES REP: *(Problem's-outcome identifying question)* "Let me see what it's costing you then to treat post-operative complications over the course of six months. It comes to $57000; how does that sound?" *(severe problem's outcome over time)*

CUSTOMER: "I didn't realize that we pay that much." *(great recognition developing for the problem's outcomes)*

SALES REP: Wish creation "Yes, you are, In terms of implementation of the technique, how does this impact the anesthesia time?"

CUSTOMER: "It takes about 20 minutes to implement." *Customer should start to recognize the prolonged anesthesia time (problem's outcome over time)*

SALES REP'S ANSWER #1: "That means that using the existing technique, *(Problem)* the anesthesia time takes 20 minutes just to implement, and as you know that 20 minutes is enough to drop body temperature below 37 C which puts the patient at *(problem's impact)* risk of developing hypothermia which then *(outcome of a problem's impact)* triples the risk of surgical site infections. *(awareness)* That's exactly what has compelled the other accounts to add more irrigation fluids to overcome hypothermia. "How do you view the impact of hypothermia and its cost to reverse?" *This is how you create wishes by avoiding hypothermia and its complications*

SALES REP'S ANSWER #2: "Our new technique can be implemented in two minutes which would be more convenient for the staff." *The sales rep. jumped in to step 3 which is presenting his product with no mention yet of an extra valued feature's impact and outcome.*

THE CUSTOMER'S RESPONSE TO THE SALES REP'S FIRST ANSWER: "Yes, this is one of the problems and in addition, we need to provide more irrigation fluids to maintain body temperature." *(The sales person succeeds in getting the customer to realize what the problem's impact and related outcome is by using an awareness statement). Greater recognition is developing now.*

What happened here?

The sales representative was successful in increasing awareness about an existing problem with the other accounts and creating the anticipated *wishes* and relating them to product's impact, outcome and value, which is why the customer recognized the solution to solve the problem's impacts and related outcomes.

THE CUSTOMER'S ANSWER TO THE SALES REP'S SECOND ANSWER: "Our staff are accustomed to the invasive technique and don't have a problem with the set up." Watch out – you've almost lost the sales call.

What happened here?

The sales rep didn't use an awareness statement, so the customer didn't realize the problem's impact or create a customer *wish* and thus couldn't relate the value and its impact and outcome to a *wish*. Instead, he focused only on the need for a new technique *(red flag raised here because of the word NEW)* which already exists regardless of the implementation time. *(The customer in this scenario didn't recognize the wish/value relationship.)*

Wishes may include the following:

A non-invasive technique *(a feature and a wish)*, which reduces anesthesia time *(an impact)*, reduces the amount of irrigation fluids *(an outcome)*, and reduces costs *(a value)*.

A non-invasive technique *(a feature and a wish)*, which reduces implementation time *(an impact)*, thus eliminating the risk of causing hypothermia *(an outcome)* and as a result reduces surgical site infections to a third of what they would otherwise be *(an outcome)* which then typically reduces both the length of a hospital stay *(a value)* and the post-operative costs *(a value)*.

> SALES REP: *(Solution-input question)* "We have offered a great solution *(meaning, a better product or improved technique or process)* which has helped similar hospital accounts reduce post-operative costs, minimize anesthesia time and save the hospital the expense of having to use more irrigation fluids, while using a technique that is 99.9% as accurate as the invasive technique. How does that sound?" *(Awareness statement about a solution for similar accounts and relate values to wishes.)*
>
> CUSTOMER: "Sounds good. How long would it take to set that up?" *(This is a buying signal.)*
>
> SALES REP: "It takes only two minutes *(Easy implementation)*, which decreases implementation time by 18 minutes (a wish), which would be more convenient to use and set up *(a wish)* and as a result there is reduced anesthesia time *(a wish)* and the risk of surgical site infections is reduced by 99.9% *(impact)*. Post-operative costs are saved *(value)*

and the cost of irrigation fluids is also reduced *(value)*. *(Pause: Relate value to customer wishes, impact, present and easy implementation of the new solution, and pause to give the customer the chance to think and engage more.)*

CUSTOMER: "What about the accuracy? Any studies done to assess that?" *(A buying signal)*

SALES REP: "That's a great question. I completely agree about the importance of supporting studies." *You've made a support intervention.* "The product is FDA-approved with 26 trials published in the American medical journal. FDA studies show a 99.9% accuracy rate compared to the invasive technique and the system has been implemented in 13 major hospitals in the US so far with great appreciation from all staff members." At this point, provide the customer with a list of peers elsewhere who are using the product. "Would that be something you'd be interested in trying and then you could see how much your patients would benefit from the system?" *Start to implement. So, you've made a support intervention, clarified and begun to implement your solution.*

CUSTOMER: "You can arrange a trial with our operating room manager next week."

That is an example of a real sales situation I was coaching with a sales professional at Edwards Lifesciences who successfully got the customer to identify the problems, create *wishes* and recognize the values offered. The sale closed for $225,000 as an initial order after executing a successful trial.

Until the deal reaches this step, the sale is not closed yet. Why? Because part of the success relies also on how you execute your demo and trial but at least you have reached 75% of the way to the close.

Common objections in the Presentation stage

Feature/ impact/outcome/value exercise for the Presentation Step:

Once you detect the problems, their impacts and outcomes, you then start converting customer *wishes/needs* through real solutions using your product features and impacts, outcomes and values.

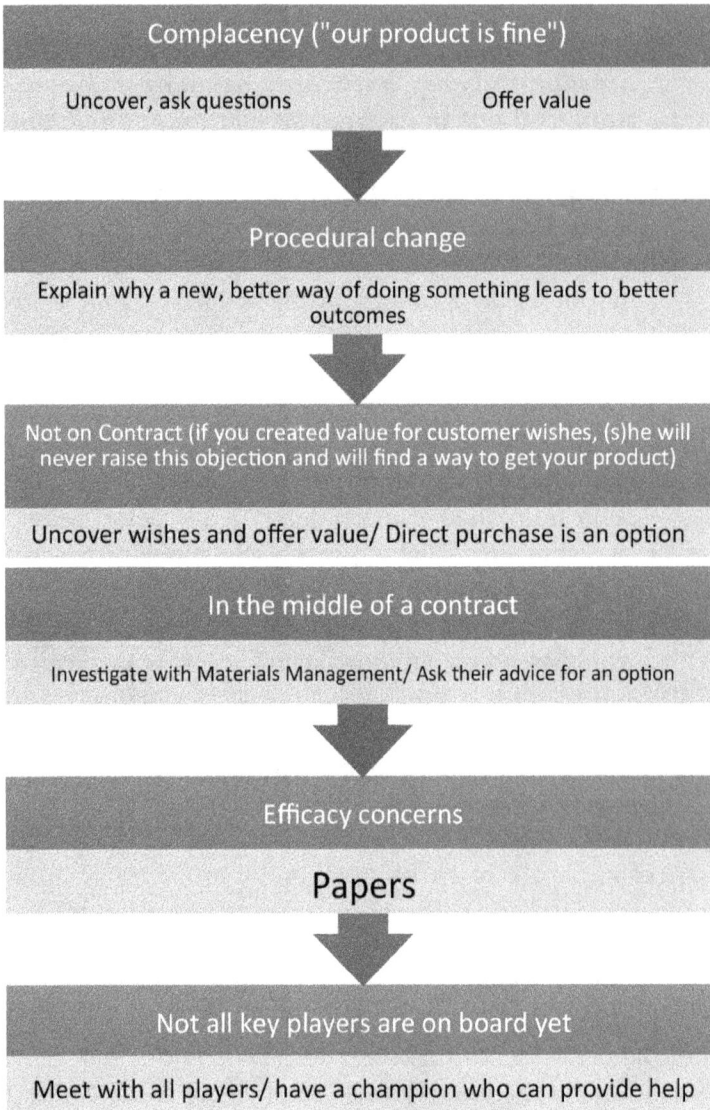

FIOV examples:

Non-invasive		
Feature	Impact	Outcome and value
Minimally-invasive technique	Reduce surgical site infections	Reduce hospital stay and post-operative complications and cost

Sensor-replacing invasive catheter		
Feature	Impact	Outcome and value
Using a sensor to monitor heart hemodynamics	1. Easy setup 2. Reduced setup time	1. More staff convenience 2. Reduce anaesthesia time and hypothermia complications 2. Reduce amount of irrigation fluids needed and save costs

Another example

Suppose you are presenting a foam surgical instrument cleaner which has a neutral PH and is blue in color.

Foamy instrument cleaner

Foam instrument cleaner		
Feature	Impact	Outcome and value
Foamy spray	No splashing chemical hazard	Safer for the staff and reduces infections

Neutral PH

Cleaner has neutral PH		
Feature Neutral PH	Impact No corrosive action on the instrument	Outcome and value Longer instrument life and reduced cost

Blue-colored foam

Blue Foam Instrument Cleaner		
Feature Blue in color	Impact Visual evidence of full coverage of the instrument	Outcome and value Ensures full cleaning of the instrument and reduces infection-related costs

Mentioning the features and using the word 'benefits' doesn't mean anything to the customer. Don't assume that the customer understands your intervention's impact, outcomes and values. You should practice this approach for every product you have in your portfolio.

Impacts / beneficiaries relationship

We have learned to always mention the feature and corresponding impact, but we need to differentiate between the feature's impact on the patient and its impact on the customer.

Example:

> SALES REP: "This system is minimally invasive, so it reduces the risk of surgical site infections by 99.9%."

In this sentence the sales rep mentioned the feature and its impact upon the patient, but there is another beneficiary: guess who? The customer is the other beneficiary. The impact is the result of your

solution implementation in which the customer benefits from reduced costs. That's what we call value, and, in this case, it is a dual value: both the patient and your customer benefit. Some features have more than one impact and more than one value: for the end user or the customer.

Once you have presented your features, impacts and outcomes, you need to get commitment to proceed to the next step.

> SALES REP: "How does that sound?"
>
> CUSTOMER: "It sounds good, but what kind of costs are involved?"
>
> SALES REP: "If we look at the price difference between our product and a similar one on the market, adding in the value of being able to avoid splashing chemical hazards and the related costs of that, plus ensuring full cleaning of the medical instruments, as well as longer instrument life and its related turnover cost, you will find the cost difference between our detergent and other detergents on the market is negligible."
>
> CUSTOMER: "How can we be sure that the product really fits what we are looking for?"
>
> SALES REP: "The best way to know that is to do a demo and a trial, and that's how you make sure that the product meets your expectations."
>
> CUSTOMER: "Sure, how about next week?"

Remember that mentioning the cost of the product before doing a demo and trial is not advisable. Always try to leave the price negotiation until after this step.

From our research into 250 sales calls in medical device sales, we found that most successful calls involved conducting the trial first *before negotiating the price*. Your negotiating power will be stronger position after you've conducted a successful product trial.

Negotiating the price:

If the customer insists on knowing the exact price before doing the demo or trial, it's fine to reveal the price but very important to *focus only on the price difference* between your product and the competitor's product. Don't focus on the list price. Instead, break down the price difference versus outcomes and values in case of a price objection.

POSTPONE NEGOTIATING THE PRICE UNTIL AFTER YOUR PRODUCT TRIAL

Example: Focus on the price difference

If you are trying to sell a product which has a price tag of $100,000 and your competitor's price is $80,000, you should always focus on the $20,000 difference rather than the $100,000 price tag, because your customer already knows that there is a minimum cost of $80,000 to purchase the competing product anyway. You need to sell the impacts, outcomes and values behind the $20,000 difference.

It's a common mistake that sales professionals sometimes focus on selling a $100,000 product but fail to pay attention to the extra money the customer will pay. This will be a chance to minimize the objection that the customer might raise regarding the list price.

Customers in purchasing departments always shop around to get at least three offers to submit to their management. It's a common practice in facilities. Do your best to find out who your competitors are and what their prices are.

Management most often looks for the best offer and rarely considers the values behind the price differences, so it's crucial to highlight the extra feature's impacts, outcomes and values that underlie any price difference and how they could improve the outcomes either for patients or for your customer's practice.

If you try to determine your competitor's price from your customer, you are not likely to obtain the information. The customer usually has an obligation to act in a fair and neutral manner with all vendors during the buying process and thus cannot reveal a competitor's pricing to you, or your pricing to your competitors.

Example:

Let's say the customer asks:

> CUSTOMER: "How much does this product cost?"
> SALES REP: The product price is $60,000 but if we look at actually how much you pay it amounts to a $20,000 difference

between our product and the other product, as you will pay at least $40,000 for any of them anyway.

SALES REP: "For a $20,000 price difference, we reduce the risk of surgical site infections by 99.9% and reduce post-operative complications, reduce the length of a hospital stay and as a result reduce post-operative costs which actually saves you more than $20,000 a year. The price difference only comes to $330 per month over the course of five years depreciation.

By responding in this way, you converted the difference that the customer pays into a saving.

The same situation applies if you are offering two products with different prices. One of them has a price of $2000 while the other performs the same function but has more features and has a price of $2500. You should focus on the outcomes and values of that $500 price difference.

8

Demo and Trial stage

*B*efore setting your product's demo and trial stage. You should ask very important questions before conducting the product demo and trial.

- What is the current process or protocol needed to conduct a product demo?
- Who is going to approve it?
- Do you need to ask permission from the group purchasing organization (GPO)?
- What are they using right now?
- What is the current satisfaction level for the existing product in use?
- How many people are involved in the decision to commence a trial?
- Which of the decision makers will declare the trial a success or failure, and is that one person or a group of people?
- What kind of training is needed for the staff during the trial?

It's crucial to know if you are the only vendor conducting a demo and trial or if some other competitors will do a trial as well. If other competitors will be conducting a demo and trial, it's important to know what their trial product is. You might determine this information in the early stage of the sales process or before the demo stage.

If your demo and trial is going to take place at around the same time as a competitor's demo and trial is also taking place, it's important to study your competitor's product thoroughly, as in the demo stage you need to focus on the strengths of your product compared with your competitor's. Furthermore, it's best if your demo and trial *starts after* your competitor's demo and trial, because you will have the opportunity to glean the customer's impressions about your competitor's products, identify any of its weaknesses, and seal the deal for your product.

FOR A SUCCESSFUL TRIAL, SET OPTN GUIDELINES WITH YOUR CUSTOMER IN ADVANCE

Setting OPTN guidelines for product trials with your customer:

Here is a very important step you need to setup before going ahead doing the demo and trial.

1. Set trial Objective(s) and goals with the customer.
2. Set Parameters of a successful trial.
3. Set a Timeline for the trial (increase time period to break customer : problem bonds).
4. Set the Next step after the trial's success, which is the quote and preparing the purchase order (P.O).

> **Product trial process into facility**
>
> - What is the process to bring trial product(s) into the facility?
> - Is this question for supply chain or purchasing?

> **Uncover person's role in decision making process**
>
> - Current supplier, current product details, level of current satisfaction, potential for change
> - How many people are involved in the decision to commence a trial?
> - Which program and products are they using presently?
> - What kind of feedback has the customer had from staff regarding the current program?

> **Uncover the type of training and needs**
>
> - What type of training does your customer want his/her staff to receive during the trial?
> - If a trial is to take place, what do we need to know about?

The execution of the demo and then executing the trial are very important steps in your sales cycle success. We found from our research that many sales professionals don't set guidelines for their trial with the customer and the results are poor, with the sales rep likely to lose the trial opportunity and the sale. In the following, you can see the product trial guidelines (OPTN) which consists of 4 steps. The data for trial success is analyzed as follows:

Taking the commitment for the next step represents 25% of your trial success, setting the parameters of trial success represents 40% of your trial's success, 15% depends on setting trial objectives and 20% on setting the time line, each.

Setting OPTN guidelines usually takes place with the person in charge of the trial, such as the OR manager, or ICU manager. Failing to set these can ruin your chances of securing a sale.

In our research of 470 trials, the trial success rate was approximately 85% upon setting OPTN trial guidelines with customers, and only a 15% success rate without setting them.

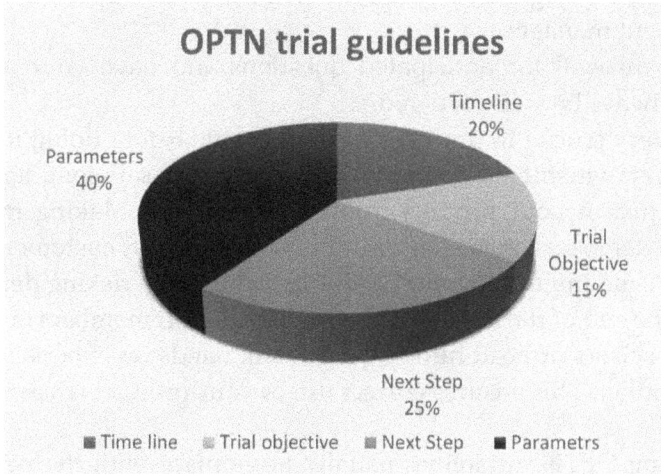

Step 4: Demo stage

In the demonstration stage you show the customer how your product works, your product strengths, instructions for use and you explain any important precautions that need to be mentioned.

Factors governing a successful demo.

1. Know which staff members will attend the demo before executing the trial.
2. You should be present during all staff shifts to conduct the demo.
3. Prepare answers to questions you anticipate getting during your demonstrations to staff.
4. Practice doing the demo so that you can perform it flawlessly in front of the staff.
5. Ensure that the staff got hands-on experience using your product during your demo.

If you miss one shift, the staff members who didn't get the demo session might use your product incorrectly which can lead to the trial being a failure. The best way to deal with this is to prepare an attendance sheet to be signed by each staff member under supervision of the department manager.

Prepare well for anticipated questions and have your answers ready. Always be well prepared.

It's very crucial to practice the demo alone before doing it for the facility's staff members. A smooth demo gives you self-confidence and fosters trust in your product from staff members. Making mistakes during a demo leaves a negative impression and your customers could lose trust and interest in your product(s), ultimately risking demo failure. At the end of the demo make sure that all staff members or at least the supervisors or head nurses get guided, hands-on experience with your product. This ensures correct use of your product when the trial starts.

Setting OPTN guidelines usually takes place with the person in charge of the trial, such as the OR manager, or ICU manager. Failing to set these can ruin your chances of securing a sale.

Once you have completed this step with your customer, you will be ready for the trial. In some situations, the customer may issue the P.O and just skip the demo and trial step. This can happen, for example, in the case of upgrading an existing product. This depends on the customer's acceptance of the particular situation.

Step 5: Trial stage

The product Trial stage is a validation for what has been mentioned in the Presentation stage, as mentioned previously. You should establish successful trial parameters before conducting the trial and involve your service team.

Trial success rate

No
guidelines
15%

Trial
guidelines
85%

▪ Trial guidelines   ▪ No guidelines

Trial stage: attendance by sales rep.

Many sales professionals do every step very well but when the trial starts, they let it proceed without visits, relying instead on an excellently-conducted demo. They are often surprised to discover that things are going badly simply because they failed to make regular visits during the trial and weren't available to answer staff questions or to address their concerns, which might arise at any time during the trial.

It's crucial to attend the first three days of any trial, as most of the trials that fail will do so within this time frame. The most common reasons for trial failure are that 1) questions arose, or 2) the product was used improperly. If the sales rep isn't present to address the issues right at the beginning of the trial, the trial will be a failure. The customer will stop trialing the product immediately until they get answers. Sometimes the customer will call the sales rep to ask questions but, in most cases, they put your product aside and trial ends with failure, simply because the sales rep was not available.

Attending the first three days of the trial enables you to address any issue or concern on the spot. After the first three days, you can attend every other day to ensure that everything is going smoothly.

The Objective of a Trial:

Before proceeding with a product trial, you need to reconfirm the customer's objective for trying out your product. For example, if you are a sales person in Mercedes show room and you offer a customer trial on a new Mercedes car, this consists of a test drive and the objective the sales person has is to show the customer just how smoothly the engine works, for example.

Another example in medical device sales:

You have been asked to sell a set of laparoscopic equipment and instruments to one major hospital that specializes in orthopedic surgery. Your camera has excellent resolution - five times more than competing products, and yours uses a great new, minimally-invasive technique that reduces trauma and the risk of injury to zero compared with the hospital's existing equipment.

The objective should be mentioned to the customer.

Objective: To compare camera resolution and to show proof of lower risk to surgical patients using your laparoscopic system versus the equipment that the customer is presently using.

Parameters for trial success in this example:

1. Showing clearer camera image on the monitor compared to what the customer is using.
2. Showing how convenient the minimally invasive technique is compared to the existing product in reducing trauma, for example - by using a different trocar and cannula.
3. Showing the high-quality color resolution on the monitor.

By setting the objective and parameters with your customers, it allows them to see the how your product is superior to what they're using, and they can thus see that the trial has been a success.

Parameters for a Trial's success:

Integral with the trial's objective, in the previous example of a new Mercedes car, are the parameters of test drive success, as follows:

Objective: customer judgment on engine smoothness and performance.

Parameters for successful customer's judgment on the test drive would be:

- Noisiness of the engine on the road.
- Engine performance from low speed to high speed.
- Transmission performance related to engine noise.
- Engine noise when accelerating from 0 to 100 km.

If the sales person sets up the objective and parameters with the customer before the test drive, then this ensures maximum customer satisfaction which ends with the sale closing successfully.

Imagine you went to a Mercedes showroom and you liked a car and then the salesperson asks you to do a test drive without establishing the objective and the parameters you would consider. What would your reaction be as a customer? You might simply reply, 'No, it's ok, no need.'

This customer could leave the Mercedes showroom and go for BMW and if the BMW sales person was successful in setting the test drive's (the trial's) objectives and criteria for success (parameters), if the test drive results aligned with what has been set by the salesperson, the customer will sign the sale contract, and the deal will be closed with BMW.

Ultimately, Mercedes loses the sale because there were no clear objectives or parameters for the test drive mentioned to the customer.

The same rules apply for every sales situation.

A Trial's time frame:

The duration of a product trial varies depending upon the customer's preference. If you are trialing capital equipment or a new system, two weeks is usually selected. However, you will want to extend the trial if the customer presently uses a competitor's product. Why? You should extend the product trial to create a new bond between your customer and your product (a new solution with an added impact/ outcome and value) and break your customer's bond with the existing product made by your competitor. This was explained previously as a customer : problem bond.

Step 6: Closing the Deal.

Close and pre-commitment for the P.O (purchase order)

You and your customer agreed about preparing the P.O. upon the trial's success. This is one of the most important steps in preparing for your demo and trial (one of OPTN trial guidelines).

Getting the P.O. is the final process which is a result of executing every step in the sales process successfully by getting commitment after each step to proceed with the following step.

Price negotiations:

Price negotiations are usually initiated by the buyers after a successful trial in preparation for the purchase order. As previously mentioned, decision makers ask about the price during your presentation, but it's crucial to postpone discussion of pricing until after the trial. This increases the likelihood that staff members and decision makers will form a strong bond with you / your product without the price influencing their opinion.

Buyers always ask for discounts - that's very common - and they ask how much discount you can provide. Initially you will be provided with a fixed product price from your company, based on quantity. There are two or three prices: a price for minimum quantities, a price for medium quantities and a price for large quantities. When you start negotiating the price, the first question you should ask should be about the estimated consumption per month and then calculate it per year.

You need to point out to your buyers, that the most economical situation for them is to order what they need and to keep a minimum stock level for 3 months. Don't be pushy to try to get them to order in bulk because it could result in returns due to the expiration date (if your products have a short expiry date).

If you can secure a P.O for a six-month supply or a one-year supply, it will be a great win and you can make a scheduled delivery as needed. You can tempt the customer by giving the best price after your management's approval, wait for one or two days and provide your best price written in an agreement or a quotation form to be approved. Securing a six-month supply or a one-year supply is advantageous to you as well since it helps you with estimating and forecasting your future plans, identifying pipeline opportunities and revenues that will be generated for this period of time. Management likes to see these kinds of sales.

The quotation form must indicate the quantities, special price, validity time of the quotation, estimated delivery date, code number of the product (s), description of the product, warranty, terms and method of payment.

If your buyer notes that the P.O might take a while to consume given what is left from an existing product, you need to ask about the quantity of the existing product in use and perhaps you will decide to buy out this stock if it has reasonable value and to make a credit note from your first purchase order equal the same amount (in cost). If this is not applicable, you can suggest making the P.O. with a scheduled delivery time.

As a general rule, don't offer any discount without reason. You offer a quality product which has a great value, and the customer needs to pay for that. You must assess the situation based on the quantities and continuity of the business relationship.

At the start of any new business relationship, buyers always assess the success of your company based on your company's customer service. After-sale services include your commitment to deliver on time, the quality of the product, the absence of complaints from the end user(s), and your continuous efforts to retain the customer's business and provide the best service. The role of inside sales reps is important at this level of communications as well, as this will make your customers rest assured that they will be able to get any information they need in a timely manner.

The key in any business relationship is to respond as quickly as possible to any inquiry.

You as a sales professional along with your inside sales team have a great responsibility to encircle your customers, keep them satisfied, maintain a great relationship so they will never look for a new company to provide the products/services that you provide so well.

By contrast, expect customers to look for products or services from your competitor if you neglect them after the sale is made, fail to respond to their inquiries, or fail to communicate or miscommunicate any information they might need.

Step 7: In-service

After getting your P.O., the implementation process begins with an in-service. In this process you need to explain all the technical details how the product works and fits into the customer's practice so that it is part of the daily practice. In this step, the customer wants to know every single detail about the product's use and setup, precautions, side effects, etc. Usually the department manager gathers the staff members and makes an appointment with you to provide more details about the product. Be prepared for questions related to the implementation process.

Post-call analysis:

Post-call analysis is a very important step for improving your professionalism. Analyze your call and find out what worked well and what didn't, what you asked and what you should ask again next time and what you asked that need not be asked again. What was the customer's reaction to your presentation? Did you gain a great commitment or not? Write down your customer's questions and any concerns which you weren't able to answer and set out to find out those answers. Were you able to identify your customer's needs and wishes and were you able to satisfy them? What did you learn about this customer during the call?

Step 8: Asking for referrals

This is an ongoing process. You should have regular customer visits after the in-service, as it gives a good impression to the customer in terms of good after-sale support. During your regular visits, you should ask for referral. A satisfied customer will be pleased to refer you to another customer.

9
Exercises

Exercise: A pharmaceutical sale.

Role play scenarios 1:

You have a new product launch for an anti-hypertensive drug which has fewer side effects than the competitor's drug, and yours works through a new mechanism of action which makes it more potent.

Your customer:

Dr. James is a very busy cardiologist who is on your customer list but has never prescribed any product from your company before. It's the first sales call. You tried to set an appointment through his administrative assistant, but she told you that the doctor is very busy and cannot meet with you.

Who are you?

You are a newly-hired sales representative in the company and you have a list of potential customers. Dr. James is one of them.

Task:

What's your strategy for successfully securing a meeting with him or what could you could have done in order to get a meeting with him?

- Design a one-page brochure
- Prepare for your call.
- Present your product to Dr. James.
- Get the commitment and close the sale.

Work with your colleagues to sell your product using the guidelines in this book and apply them to working with Dr. James.

In the same scenario:

You were successful in getting a meeting with Dr. James. Right after your attention grabber, he gave you five minutes to do your call, and he doesn't want to engage. What's your strategy to get him more engaged and then get his commitment?

Scenario 2:

You are presenting a new product for type 2 diabetes. Your product offers new advantages over your competitor's product in terms of efficacy and dose convenience.

Your customer:

Dr. Vicki is a diabetes specialist, and she has an old practice. She has prescribed your company's products in the past but has stopped prescribing them in the last two years.

Who are you?

You are handed over a new territory and Dr. Vicki is one of the potential customers in your list.

During your chat with the nearest pharmacy, you discover that Dr. Vicki has been prescribing two competitors' products for her diabetic patients during the past 2 years.

You were successful in getting Dr. Vicki's admin assistant to set up a *lunch and learn* for you and Dr. Vicki.

Task:

At the start of your call, Dr. Vicki said very little but showed some hostility when you started probing. You can ask her to describe her relationship with your company over the past few years.

Design a two-page for your sales call.

- What are you going to prepare before making your sales call.
- What's your new strategy for this sale call now that you see that she is hostile?
- How do you present your product?
- Take the commitment and close.

Take time with your team members to role-play how you intend to do the sales call. Have fun

Scenario 3

You are presenting an established hormonal replacement therapy (already on the market for five years) and you are re-launching it with a new supporting study about fewer side effects for hysterectomized patients compared to what was published three years ago.

Your customer

Dr. Carrie is a very busy gynecologist. She was a heavy prescriber of your drug three years ago for intact uterus patients and switched to a natural product but sometimes she still prescribes your drug.

Who are you?

Experienced sales specialist. You know Dr. Carrie from before as a skeptical personality and she set aside only 15 minutes to meet with you.

Tasks

- Prepare for your call. Prepare an introduction and attention grabber. Be prepared for your probing questions. What are you going to focus on during your presentation?
- Close and get the commitment.

Complex sale scenarios:

Scenario:

You are asked to sell a set of laparoscopic equipment and instruments to one major hospital that specializes in orthopedic surgery. Your camera has excellent resolution - five times more than competing products, and yours uses a great new, minimally-invasive technique that reduces trauma and the risk of injury to zero compared with the hospital's existing equipment. Your product costs 20% more than the hospital's existing product.

Your customer

The department of surgery is your customer. The hospital buys through an RFP process and is concerned about price and rarely places a direct order.

Who are you?

You are a medical device sales territory manager. You have never sold this type of equipment before, but you are well-trained in sales.

Your Task:

- Prepare the attention grabber.
- Prepare for the awareness statement and related probing questions.
- Present your product.
- Be ready for two objections (they buy through RFPs and they have price objections).
- Set the OPTN guidelines.
- Close the sale

Self-Assessment and Sales Pitch Exercises

Exercise: wishes, needs and wants:

Need	Wish	Want
I need to buy a house	I wish to buy a house on a corner lot (pay more)	I want white tiles in the kitchen
I need to buy a car	I wish to have leather seats (pay more)	I want to have it in red color

Feature, impact, outcome and value exercise (FIOV):

If you are already a sales rep, select a few of your products and identify the feature, impact, outcome and value of each of those selected products. If you are new to sales, think of a common product, such as cars, and practice identifying the feature, impact, outcome and value to various customers visiting the dealership.

Feature	Impact	Outcome	Value

Concluding Remarks

Sales success is a result of many elements coming together. This group of elements represents a chain that includes leadership skills, earning your customer's confidence by establishing a history of multiple effective encounters and events with your customer, identifying customer's issues and challenges and offering ways to resolve them, excellent presentation and professional selling skills, and effective communication skills.

You now have an effective method for dealing with every sort of sales situation, from the simplest to the most challenging, and it applies to both simple and complex sales. You know how to sell to customers presently using a competitor's product or who are looking to implement a totally new solution. You know how to approach each sort of customer personality for best results, and how to prepare for sales meetings and how to follow-up with prospects and existing customers. Using the APWS Selling Method, you will have the best chance of securing a purchase order and repeat sales from your customers and, of course, of meeting your sales targets each year. Only a systematic approach like the one described here will get you consistent good results. Use it for every customer, and be honest with yourself and critical of how well you followed each step to determine if there are areas in which you need to improve. Use the exercises in this book as starting points, and create a template/checklist for yourself to use for each account and each prospective account to ensure that you've done everything you can to succeed as a sales professional in pharmaceutical sales, medical device sales or whatever industry you work in.

Appendix

Leadership and Functional Competencies

A sales team is the most effective tool for success in any company, and there are several skills that must be in place for sales professionals to be successful.

Some of the most important skill sets are leadership and functional competencies.

The leadership model needed to drive sales can effectively be classified into the six components:

LEADERSHIP MODEL

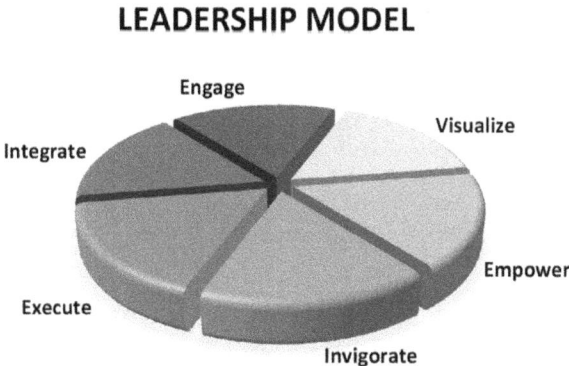

Engage

Visualize

Integrate

Empower

Execute

Invigorate

The definition for each leadership component should be clarified by sales managers, business unit managers and supervisors of the sales professionals. This model represents a set of expectations by leaders to assess sales performance.

Visualize: details how the sales professional sees and shares a path to the future.

Empower: demonstrates how the sales professional enables others to do their best work.

Invigorate: demonstrates how the sales professional inspires and energizes others and helps build a strong team.

Execute: refers to the ability of the sales professional to carry out and accomplish what (s)he planned for, i.e., to consistently and safely deliver results, exhibiting a competitive drive to win and an exceptional work ethic.

Integrate: demonstrates an accountability towards the company's culture and values, fitting in well with the company's environment and being a part of the company 'family'.

Engage: details the ability of the sales professional to engage with other people and the ability to engage people with them, communicate effectively, and the ability to build rapport with people and the ability to build long lasting relationships.

Most companies look for these components and related competencies when sales professionals are evaluated.

Sales managers:

> *"Always treat your employees exactly
> as you want them to treat your best
> customers."*[1]

> *"Effective management is putting first
> things first. While leadership decides what
> "first things" are, it is management that
> puts them first, day-by-day, moment-
> by-moment. Management is discipline,
> carrying it out."*[2] *(Steven Covey)*

Leadership is not about instructing people to do what they should or shouldn't do. It's about leading a team to success, and the key to a team's success involves:

- trusting the team's abilities to do tasks
- understanding the mentality of each team member
- getting closer to each member and understanding what kind of management style each one likes or dislikes
- being a good listener to learn their needs
- dealing with matters fairly and,
- refraining from nitpicking over mistakes.

Instead, sales leaders can provide constructive feedback about mistakes, and always praise a job well done. Praise has a magical influence on motivation and inspires better performance.

> *Involve your team in every challenge and
> work out the solution together.*

Why do excellent sales performers leave organizations and look for another job? Most studies indicate the main reason for leaving is their manager's management style and behavior.

Salespeople become very disillusioned when they discover that their sales managers don't honor their promises.

There are also other reasons for leaving bad managers, including:

1. Managers may lack faith in their team's ability to perform tasks and they may micromanage their sales reps, especially if the salespeople are professionals.
2. Managers fail to praise their staff for their achievements.
3. Managers overlook some team members which leads the overlooked members to wonder if there is some form of discrimination present.
4. Managers may nitpick sales staff for their mistakes and fail to offer constructive feedback.
5. Managers sometimes underestimate the sales team's skills.
6. Managers involve themselves in deals and take the credit for themselves.
   Salespeople prefer managers who give clear guidance, set clear objectives and, give clear and honest feedback about each salesperson's performance.

In one situation, a sales professional was working in a multinational company, and he told me that his direct manager was getting his weekly reports and deleting any negative comments or suggestions to correct any negative point in the sales person's reports before submitting the report to the vice-president of sales and marketing. His direct manager was doing the same thing every week. The end result was that the sales professional resigned 6 months after he was hired. It's an example of unethical conduct.

In another case, a different sales professional told me why he resigned despite having been the top performer for six months, always successfully managing sales situations on his own. His direct sales manager started demanding to be copied on all the salesman's emails to customers. Soon thereafter, the salesman realized that his manager was contacting the salesman's customers without informing him, leaving the salesman in the dark as to what was happening with his own customers. The end result was that the salesman became disconnected from his customers and he decided to resign. This is an example of management not trusting its sales professionals to manage their accounts, and it amounts to constructive dismissal.

Unhealthy Pressure:

Most sales managers get pressured by top management to achieve sometimes unrealistic forecasts, which can reflect increases of 20% to

30% year-over-year without even adding any new products or having enough opportunities in the pipeline. In return, some sales managers simply pass the unrealistic quota to their team. This can be very frustrating and can fuel failure for all. As a result, sales managers have an excuse to lay off one or two of their team members or they are advised by upper management to lay off one or two to reduce costs so as to compensate for modest achievements in the face of the new, unrealistic forecast.

In some situations, some sales managers increase sales target percentages in a non-uniform manner, assigning an unreasonable percentage to some but not all the salespeople, which can be very frustrating for the whole team and could be the beginning of the team's eventual failure. Furthermore, it can create a significant level of dissatisfaction between team members and could be the main reason for team members - even the best performers - to look for employment elsewhere.

Sales managers or business unit managers need to be very careful setting the forecasts, and percentage increases should be aligned with the general strategy of their division. Forecasts should be based on:

- the size of the area
- opportunities in the pipeline
- the number of new prospects
- any new product added and its segment within the market share
- market growth and its reasonable percentage
- previous area performance, and
- the territory representative's performance as well.

Functional Competencies

There are seven functional competencies considered to be integral parts of the leadership model which must be considered to evaluate a salesperson's level of proficiency and success.

Customer versatility

Customer versatility is the ability of the sales professional to perceive and respond appropriately to different customer situations and environments, and to effectively interact with a variety of customer contacts at different levels and within different departments throughout any given facility.

Customer relationship development

In this competency, the sales professional is able to develop effective customer relationships by establishing trust based on competence, integrity, industry best practices and customer knowledge at any healthcare facility and departmental levels. The sales professional is knowledgeable about how the customer's organization operates, along with the goals and priorities of the customer.

Strategic account management

The ability of the sales professional to plan and execute a strategic approach to sell a broad pipeline of products, services and programs.

Technical Aptitude

Demonstrates the ability and interest to learn clinical healthcare industry trends, terminology and processes, exhibit motivation and skill to gather, analyze and deduce meaningful conclusions from data.

Internal partnership development

This competency pertains to the ability of the salesperson to identify all of his or her company's skills and resources, and to build relationships with fellow employees, so as to fully utilize the company's offerings in fostering maximal growth for the company while simultaneously giving customers every benefit that the company can provide its customers.

Executional excellence

Consistently delivers on all aspects of selling and servicing the customer base. Establishes clear goals, plans and timelines for purposeful activity, and achieves sales goals by applying proven sales strategies and tactics.

Learning agility

Readily learns and adopts new products, tools, processes, programs and technology.

The job of a sales professional in the healthcare industry is multi-faceted, requiring both a technical understanding of healthcare as well as exceptional interpersonal skills to develop effective customer relationships. Time, training and commitment are needed to fully develop the skills to be effective.

Leadership and functional competencies evaluation
Sales professional Functional Competency Assessment

What you'll need:

This is an assessment that can be done by a sales manager for their team. Sales Managers can describe the competency name, definitions and assess the degree of professionalism in each competency for every member of the team.

Directions:

For each competency, review the competency definition and descriptions, then assess your team's proficiency in each of the three stages: on a scale from 1 to 10 (10 is high and 1 is low), learning, experienced or mastery.

Functional competency	Learning	Experienced	Mastery
Customer versatility			
Customer relationship development			
Strategic account management			
Technical aptitude			
Internal partnership development			
Executional excellence			
Learning agility			

Sales professional career progression

Sales professionals are classified in multinational companies based on their level of competence.

Learning stage

In this stage, you are newly-hired, and you need some time to become fully aware of all the details of your company products, the reporting system, the company's internal system, and communication channels. During the first year or two in your sales position, you will need to:

- get to know your boss and co-workers' working style, how your company's system operates, tasks need to be completed before going for actual selling in the field, different communication channels inside the company, and perhaps inside politics, especially in the first 3 to 6 months, that's a very important part of your success.
- identify your potential customers in your territory and build up your customer's trust and confidence.
- classify customers in your territory based on their potential, and,
- learn more about each customer's practice and their obstacles to offer your best solutions.

Experienced Stage

In this stage, you demonstrate competence in customer relationship development and strategic account management, as well as the ability to establish clear goals and plans within the specified timeline. This period may last from two to four years, depending upon the sales professional's competencies and his or her achievements to date. Such achievements include how well the sales professional is managing customer accounts (e.g., clinics, hospitals) and how well the sales professional is developing positive customer relationships.

Mastery Stage

In this stage, a sales professional demonstrates executional excellence in all competencies. It generally takes more than four or five years of experience to reach this level of mastery.

Goal setting

One of the most important steps in achieving goals depends on your commitment and persistence to achieve them. Goals may be set more than one time, once in the beginning of the year, revised every six months or every quarter. Sales professionals should refrain from setting more than four goals, as having too many goals can make it impossible to achieve any of them.

Goals can be classified into three main categories:

PERSONAL GOALS: Whether they are short or long-term goals, companies want to see what your vision of your future is. They want to know how you plan to improve your current situation such that it results in a win - win situation. Taking a course to improve a skill or enrolling in a program that would be beneficial to your sales role are examples of short-term goals that benefit both you and your company.

Long-term personal goals must be set in order to have a clear vision for your future. You can set your career path objectives, especially if you are a new graduate. These include, 'what do I really want to be?', 'how do I achieve it?' 'What do I need to do to achieve my goal?' 'How long will it take?' 'Is it worth it to pursue this path?'

For sales professionals, it is crucial to set long-term goals, whether for personal life goals or career advancement.

It's important to assess the current situation. What are your real weaknesses and how can you improve? Who could help you to improve? How long might it take? What would you like to be in the future?

Setting goals and knowing how to execute plans to achieve one's goals is a broad subject and will be explained in a separate book, which will be available soon.

SALES GOALS. One of the most important steps is to focus on setting no more than three or four main goals. This will help you to focus on planning and executing. For example:

- Achieve sales forecast for specific indication in certain groups of patients.
- Create sales leads for a specific drug by participating in major conferences.
- Set a marketing plan and detail how to execute it.

- Conduct three product trials from a specific product in six months.
- Implement a program in a certain period of time.

This should be aligned with your company's vision and strategy. You need to specify a time line to achieve each goal and identify the tactics you will use to achieve each one.

Tactics include your action plan to achieve your goals and objectives. For example, gathering information about customer prescribing behavior, completing your training modules, your business plan, your routing plan; info about your competitors; preparing for your product sales call which includes your attention grabber, probing questions, anticipated objections and their answers; tactics for dealing with different behaviors and personalities.

COMPANY VALUES AND ETHICS:

Every company has a vision, mission and code of ethics. Execution of your goals must be aligned with your company's mission, vision and code of ethics. Some of the most important company values are integrity and dedication, fair competition in the work place, avoidance of false claims and avoidance of misrepresentation. Business practices must include respect and dignity. Information must be delivered accurately and transparently. Reps must exercise good judgment, and avoid conflicts of interest. Know the 3 D's: disclose, decide and discuss. Disclosure is key.

Success drivers

To become successful in a healthcare sales career, you must pay attention to what multinational companies are looking for in terms of the responsibility of the healthcare sales professional. You are expected to develop, service and manage a territory of healthcare accounts within various market segments including hospitals and healthcare facilities; learn how each customer's facility operates; understand challenges and advise appropriate healthcare solutions; and, develop partnerships and relationships with customer/distributor networks to ensure prompt, reliable and personally-delivered service to resolve their unique healthcare concerns.

Drivers of your success

Drivers of your success include your results and their success indicators. There are five areas that every multinational company looks for when they evaluate your sales success.

Talent development

Result
Personal development

Success indicators

Willingly initiates and acts on development plan, self-motivated and anxious to learn through new experiences, takes part in action learning opportunities, focuses on self-development through continuous learning and openness to feedback.

Result

Train other team members on best practices.

Success indicators

Identify and execute actions to develop new talents, provide constructive feedback to help develop others in the team. Supportive and accepting of associates/customers who are diverse.

Leadership

Results
Influence, organizational role model, self and leadership development, strategic thinking, professionalism, self-discipline.

Success indicators

Embrace, strengthen and promote your company's culture through personal actions and team communications. Lead by example, timely follow through on promises and commitments, model ethical practices, and demonstrate integrity with others, go the extra mile with associates and customers. Use sound judgment in dealing with confidential information, self-motivated; able to work independently and manage schedule; excellent professional communication skills. Actively works to create a positive work environment for co-workers and customers.

Relationships

Results

Solid Business Relationships (Functional/Divisional), Strong Peer network (Local/National), Customer service focus, Professional communication.

Success indicators

Build and strengthen customer and networking relationships that serve to retain, grow and gain accounts, represents your company professionally and accurately all the times; trusted and respected by team, customers and management. Listen effectively and foster open communication with peers, management and customers, demonstrate professionalism in interactions and communications with others. Express ideas effectively and clearly in verbal/written communications. Ensure accessibility and responsiveness, work collaboratively with others in team.

Innovation

Results

New product development, technology use development, communication development.

Success indicators

Understand program and service protocols, leverage resources to improve performance growth and communications, leverage all resources to keep current on market, product and service data. Focus on profitability and impact of actions to organization. Focus on providing valued added services and seek unique solutions to provide proprietary advantage, readily share ideas to enhance the value of the team and organization, and display a strong curiosity for learning.

Delivering results

Results

Sales growth, service standards, professionalism, customer satisfaction, Territory management.

Success indicators

Deliver high quality individual performance to meet/exceed scorecard objectives and other targets, Work to develop new customers and grow current customer sales. Work with customers to accurately assess their needs, provide information, solve problems, and increase customer satisfaction/retention while preventing unwanted outsourcing. Understand the sales process to maximize leads and generate new business, use control/tracking system effectively to ensure quality, timely results and eliminate surprises, control expenses by managing parts inventory, collateral use and cost. Manage schedule/workload to ensure commitments are delivered on time, respond effectively to changes, Work in a safe manner and in compliance with safety regulations and legislation, understand and follow workplace safety and environmental practices and procedures.

Knowledge, skills and attributes

There are certain skills and attributes which are desirable for each success driver, as follows.

For Talent Development_

You need to be an effective and constructive communicator, have a drive to succeed, be internally motivated and self-aware.

For Leadership

You need to have confidence, be an expert in the field, be flexible, work as your company ambassador and show empathy.

For Relationships

You need to earn your customers' and your co-workers' trust. Show integrity, credibility, and build rapport. Have a collaborative mindset and good listening skills. Be perceptive, proactive, and maintain a customer-centered focus.

For Innovation

You need technical aptitude, creativity, flexibility. You need to be able to create opportunities from challenges, provide product knowledge/ service, and possess curiosity.

For Delivering Results

You need to have general business acumen, efficiency, professionalism, knowledgeable, detail oriented, good judgment, proficiency in work scope, listening and comprehension, information use, negotiation, timely, multitasking.

Communication Skills

Communication is an exchange between two persons or one involving a group of people. It requires the ability to listen, understand, speak, and interpret. Listening requires listeners to focus on what is being said and to respond accordingly.

A study by Mehrabian[3] (1971) shows the relationship between words (verbal), voice tone and body language:

Words or verbal cues in communication represent 7%, non-verbal cues like voice tone represent 38% and body language represents 55%. Effective communication starts with effective listening. Effective listening is a learned skill. Most people only listen with about 30% of their listening capacity, and they can forget or misunderstand 70% of what they hear. This means that a sale can be lost through poor listening, which could cost you and your company.

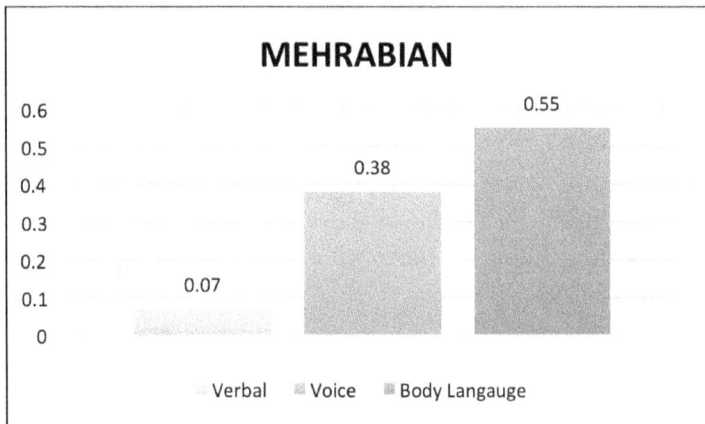

MEHRABIAN

Listening is essential in every step in the sales process, whether you are establishing rapport, probing, handling objections or closing the sale.

"Think win-win, genuine feelings for mutually beneficial solutions or agreements in your relationships. Value and respect people by understanding a "win" for all is ultimately a better long-term resolution than if only one person in the situation had gotten his way. Think Win-Win isn't about being nice, nor is it a quick-fix technique. It is a character-based code for human interaction and collaboration."[4]

Your tone of voice can make a difference

Let's take an example of a sentence like, "He didn't mention any objections about prescribing our medication." This sentence could be said in different ways depending on where you put emphasis within the sentence. Try it and take note of the different meanings that result in emphasizing different parts of the sentence.

He didn't mention any objections about prescribing our medication.
He didn't **mention** any objections about prescribing our medication.
He didn't mention **any** objections about prescribing our medication.
He didn't mention any **objections** about prescribing our medication.
He didn't mention any objections about **prescribing** our medication.
He didn't mention any objections about prescribing **our medication**.

Be sure you consider not only what you say, but how you say it, whenever you are communicating with a customer or prospective customer, whether in writing (e.g., in an email), on the phone, or in person.

BIG SHOUT OUT

This book would never have been published without the assistance of my editor, Anya Lee, (Write Results Communications, www.write-results.com), whose patience, direction, and sincere belief in my book have shaped and polished my ideas into a book that I'm proud to share with you. Anya - thanks a million for your excellent editing!

Glossary

An account: Any hospital, medical or health-related clinic or business that could or does use the sort of product that a pharmaceutical or medical device company sells is an account or a potential account.

Bioburden: Related to microbial limit testing, which is performed on pharmaceuticals and medical devices for quality control purposes. The bioburden is a measure of how much bacteria survived a sterilization process and still remains on a medical instrument after the sterilization process has been completed.

CRM: CRM is an acronym for customer relationship management. CRM lets you store and manage prospect and customer information, like contact info, accounts, leads, and managing sales opportunities in the pipeline, in one central location. You'll discover that it's not just a fancy contact list. Ultimately, a CRM solution is a game-changing piece of technology for every industry under the sun — from retail and manufacturing, to real estate, construction, and many more.

CRM can help you:

- Increase leads
- Close more deals, faster
- Drive customer loyalty and satisfaction

Gap analysis: A comparison between expectations and out-comes, between actual performance and desired or anticipated performance.

GPO: Group Purchasing Organization

Different supply chain services ensure that the right products arrive in the right location at the right time and at the best possible price. They do source from different vendors either direct purchase or through a contract.

Their services include procurement, contract management, warehousing, and their logistics teams take care of hospital supply needs.

Every chain responsible for supplying several hospitals in a specific area for their needs.

Inside Sales: Inside sales representatives are responsible for prospecting through making cold calls and identifying the potential buyers, creating sales leads and opportunities which should be followed by the outside sales team. Inside sales reps arrange paperwork for customers to establish new accounts, understand customer needs and requirements, and close uncomplicated sales.

KOL: Key Opinion Leaders

These are the persons who decide approval on your product use into the facility. KOLs may be an influencer on the purchase of your product as well. They allow a product trial to proceed and they pass judgment on your product trial and approve or disapprove the purchase of your product. They are experts in product knowledge and are trusted by the people who work closely with them. Most of the time, their final recommendations are accepted.

Prospecting:

The process of identifying potential buyers who might show an interest in your product. This process can be done by inside or outside sales staff. Once a potential buyer shows an interest in your services or products, then this buyer or customer is called a sales lead.

References

1. *Stephen R. Covey (2016). "The 7 Habits of Highly Effective People: Powerful Lessons in Personal Change Interactive Edition", p.69, Mango Media Inc.*
2. *Stephen R. Covey (2016). The 7 Habits of Highly Effective People, Stephen Covey. AZQuotes.com, Wind and Fly LTD, 2019. https://www.azquotes.com/author/3347-Stephen_Covey, accessed February 18, 2019.*
3. *Mehrabian, Albert (2009). "Silent Messages" – A Wealth of Information About Nonverbal Communication (Body Language)". Personality & Emotion Tests & Software: Psychological Books & Articles of Popular Interest. Los Angeles: self-published. Retrieved February 18, 2019.*
4. Stephen R. Covey's - The 7 Habits of Highly Effective People, *Chicago (Author-Date, 15th ed.) Covey, Stephen R. 2004. The 7 habits of highly effective people: restoring the character ethic. New York: Free Press.*
5. Neumann, Kimberly Dawn. "How Much Does Chemistry Count?". Accessed February 16, 2019. https://en.wikipedia.org/wiki/Chemistry_(relationship)
6. *Campbell, Kelly. "More Than Chemistry", a Professor of Psychology at California State University, San Bernardino. Accessed February 16, 2019.*
7. *Chemistry (personal communication), Research by Kelly Campbell, a Professor of Psychology at California State University, San Bernardino.*

8. Bo Bennett Quotes. (n.d.). BrainyQuote.com. Retrieved February 14, 2019, from BrainyQuote.com Web site: https://www.brainyquote.com/quotes/bo_bennett_167512

9. https://www.merriam-webster.com/dictionary/benefit, *accessed February 16, 2019*

10. World Bank Poverty Group on Impact Evaluation, accessed on February 11, 2019 at https://en.wikipedia.org/wiki/Impact_evaluation

11. Normative Ethics, by Shelly Kagan. Published on November 13, 1997) Paperback – https://en.wikipedia.org/wiki/Value_(ethics)

12. Mehrabian, Albert; Ferris, Susan R. (1967). "Inference of Attitudes from Nonverbal Communication in Two Channels". *Journal of Consulting Psychology*. 31 (3): 248–252. doi:10.1037/h0024648. PMID 6046577.

About the
Author

Adel Williams is the CEO and founder of Start Professional Selling and Publishing Academy Inc.

For over 25 years, he worked, built and managed effective sales teams around the world for multinational companies which included Edwards Lifesciences, Siemens Diagnostics, Covidien, Intersurgical, Ipsen Pharmaceuticals, Shoppers Drug Mart Specialty Health Network , Pfizer, Ecolab and Bard.

He developed and refined APWS as a sales professional and sales leader. His method has been used for over 57,000 sales calls over a period of four years. He possesses two graduate degrees. His book picks up where other sales books end. His insights will help sales professionals around the world attain greater sales success while giving them a proven, refined system to follow when approaching each of their customers. Motivated sales professionals now have a guide that will deliver the info that they've been seeking, all in a succinct package so that they can get on with what they love – pitching and closing a sale.